ONE WOMAN'S MIRACULOUS FACE TO FACE ENCOUNTERS WITH GOD

THE VICTORY Crown

THE MESS, THE MILLIONS, THE MIRACLES, THE MESSAGE

Joanne Hayward

First published by Ultimate World Publishing 2023
Copyright © 2023 Joanne Hayward

ISBN

Paperback: 978-1-923123-15-1
Ebook: 978-1-923123-16-8

Joanne Hayward has asserted her rights under the Copyright, Designs and Patents Act 1988 to be identified as the author of this work. The information in this book is based on the author's experiences and opinions. The publisher specifically disclaims responsibility for any adverse consequences which may result from use of the information contained herein. Permission to use information has been sought by the author. Any breaches will be rectified in further editions of the book.

All rights reserved. No part of this publication may be reproduced, stored in or introduced into a retrieval system, or transmitted in any form, or by any means (electronic, mechanical, photocopying, recording or otherwise) without the prior written permission of the author. Any person who does any unauthorised act in relation to this publication may be liable to criminal prosecution and civil claims for damages. Enquiries should be made through the publisher.

Cover design: Ultimate World Publishing
Layout and typesetting: Ultimate World Publishing
Editor: Vanessa McKay
Cover Image Copyright: Ivan Ponomarev-Shutterstock.com

Ultimate World Publishing
Diamond Creek,
Victoria Australia 3089
www.writeabook.com.au

Dedication

This book is lovingly dedicated to my Heavenly Father and Lord and Saviour, Jesus Christ. Thank you for saving me and never giving up on me. Jackson, Sarah, Gabrielle and Jerome, you are truly gifts from God and all that a mother could ever want or hope for. Lisa, you are the best big sister, and I could not have completed this book without you. Also Mum, thank you for helping us in a great time of need, I am forever grateful.

Contents

Dedication	3
Introduction	7
Chapter 1: Mucking It All Up	11
Chapter 2: The Exorcism	23
Chapter 3: It's Raining Favour	39
Chapter 4: Can I See You God?	49
Chapter 5: Face to Face with Jesus and Satan	61
Chapter 6: Be Careful What You Pray For	85
Chapter 7: Seismic Shift	101
Chapter 8: Miracles, Signs and Wonders	113
Chapter 9: Face to Face with God	123
Chapter 10: Boundaries Bring Break Through	133
Chapter 11: Nakedness Is Intimacy	143
Chapter 12: The Victory Crown	157
About the Author	167
Testimonials	169
Bibliography	171

Introduction

**"The Lord spoke to Moses face to face as
one speaks to a friend."** (Exodus 33:11)

Can a person see and speak to God face to face as they would speak to a friend? The answer is yes, and this is my story. My journey with the one and only Living God.

At 35 years old, I was an unbeliever, and my life was a complete mess. After experiencing some supernatural events, I started questioning if God was real. I prayed and asked God this question:

"Can I see you, God?"

These words were to change my life forever. I wasn't aware at that point that intimacy was what God desired. It is the most important thing we can ever do whilst on this earth.

Before my radical transformation took place, my life was quite shocking and full of crimes against God and man. Many I'd rather keep hidden, but I know that through my mess, there is a message of hope. This message is for all people, but especially for the people who have made the same mistakes I have made. People that are feeling shame and guilt, feeling like a failure, and people who are lonely and feeling unloved.

There is hope, and your mess does matter to God. He wants to bring wholeness to every part of your life. I know this because the first 35 years of my life were disastrous. Even though I had two beautiful children, I always felt like something was missing in my life. I would try to find happiness in another person or physical things in this world, but nothing could ever make me happy. There was a piece missing inside my heart and I didn't know how to fill it.

Finally, I found that missing piece. It was Jesus. I invited Jesus to come into my life and from that moment on, I have never been alone and have prospered from that day forth. Not only did He forgive me for everything I'd ever done and ever would do, but He also blessed me with two more beautiful children.

As you read this book, you will come to see that victory and prosperity look quite different through God's eyes.

My transformation took me from a single mum living in government housing to a multi-millionaire within a few short years. By buying and selling properties, I went from having nothing in the bank to owning several beachside properties worth millions. To say He blessed me is an understatement!

When I became born again at 35 years old, God went straight to work on me. When the healing was too painful to bear, I pushed through the struggles and never gave up. He helped to mature and transform me into the Godly woman He had always intended me to be, while equipping me to be of service.

My hope is that God's words of encouragement and direction, through my life's transformation, will help you overcome the setbacks in your life. It's not about running away from God when things get hard, but

Introduction

running to him as He rewards those who trust in him and depend on him.

As you read this book, I believe you will hear God's voice inspire you and help you in your own life situations. You will also receive healing from unforgiveness, hope in times of trouble, and victories from failures.

Now where there is good, there is also evil. I will also share my face-to-face encounters with Satan. I wasn't aware that demons existed until the day I became born again and my spiritual eyes opened. With God's help, I've been able to overcome every demonic attack of the enemy and come out victorious.

In this book, I'll be sharing steps to invite Jesus into your life and how you can also meet God, Jesus, and the Holy Spirit. I will also share how you too can have a personal relationship with them, and how to have a face-to-face encounter with the creator of the universe!

For I know the plans I have for you," declares the Lord, "plans to prosper you and not to harm you, plans to give you hope and a future.

JEREMIAH 29:11

Chapter 1

Mucking It All Up

**As the scriptures say,
"No one is good – not even one."**
(Romans 3:10)

As the visiting minister laid his hands upon me, my eyelids fluttered, my throat constricted and the demon that was inside me knew it had to go! As the evil departed from my innermost being, tears flowed and there was some relief, but I knew it wasn't finished yet and so did God. This was the first time I had ever felt the power of God flow through me.

The Victory Crown

"Start children off on the way they should go, and even when they are old, they will not turn from it."
(Proverbs 22:6)

From the age of six, my first memories of anything spiritual were of glowing candlesticks, statues of Mary & Jesus, and nuns hustling around with their clinking rosary beads. The only other thing that could send a shiver down my spine was the dark, confessional cupboard. After confessing my wrong doings to the hidden face behind the screen, I would have to recite a dozen Hail Marys and a dozen Our Father prayers, and it was very tedious. Years later, I would realise that this praying laid the foundations for my future salvation.

With my blonde hair and sparkling green eyes, I found great favour among the nuns in the convent, especially the older ones. You see, I had a very special knack for guessing their ages (all were twenty-one), which brought them much joy and laughter. But while I loved receiving their hugs and kisses, as the old saying goes, there's always one rotten apple.

The love I had for the nuns changed one afternoon as I watched my older sister get physically abused by one of them. Outside the old Queenslander classroom, I dashed from one window to the next, watching in horror as my sister received punches to her back and blows from a ruler on her hands, while having her head thrust back and forth by the grip on her ears. We left with our arms entwined, both of us in tears and traumatised by what had just happened. An anger rose in me against the nun who had done this and God. Thankfully, we moved away shortly after, but the memory of what had happened that day would remain with me forever.

Both my parents were young and good looking, but with my father being a local Aussie Rules football hero, it didn't take long for adultery to hit the family home. After a short separation, they reunited and started a new life in Coolum Beach, a gorgeous little beach side town on the Sunshine Coast in Queensland.

Woohoo! Sun, surf, and sand! No more hot and heavy canvas uniforms. Free dress day was every day, including no shoes, no rosary beads, no more Hail Mary and Our Father prayers. It was like I'd died and gone to school heaven. I really couldn't have been any happier. Life was good, and the beach was even better. I still went to church on Sunday and did everything a good little catholic girl should do, but it was only skin deep, and I had no clue that God was even real. I acted out of duty, not out of love for Him.

Everything was wonderful and there were many good times, especially with The Bay City Rollers and ABBA on nearly every radio station. Who wouldn't be happy? With a new best friend in tow, I was unstoppable. I was elected to be the Vice-Captain of the school for the following year in grade seven and my excitement overflowed. It was such an honour to be a leader in the last year of primary school.

Finally, a leadership position which I knew had always been in my heart.

> **"The thief comes only to steal, kill, and destroy. I have come so that they may have life and have it in all its fullness."** (John 10:10)

With no Holy Bible in the family home, I didn't realise Satan's ugly hand of destruction was about to strike me. All I knew about him I learned from my grandma. She told me that if I didn't go to sleep at her house, the devil would come and bounce on my chest. Of course, when he didn't show up for a bouncy, bouncy time, I just put it down to a figment of my granny's imagination. Boy, was I wrong!

Influenced by a friend, my mother moved me to another school for that last year of primary school. I cried, begged, and pleaded with her not to do this, but it was to no avail. I was dragged kicking and screaming to another convent over an hour away from my home and I hated it. It sent me into a downward spiral of depression, I knew no one and had no friends.

I had been stripped of my vice captaincy leadership position and been isolated from all my best friends. My spirit was broken. I went from being a happy, bubbly, cheerful little girl to a depressed and lonely outcast in a community where I knew no one.

To comfort myself I would buy take away food from the little shop next to the school, just to be cool. For the first time in my life, I was now overweight. I also developed terrible acne which made matters worse. All my confidence was gone.

God was with me and watching over me. I didn't know it, but He was always with me. I remember a small miracle happening when a nun kicked me out of my classroom and told me to go home. I left the classroom totally humiliated and started walking down a street, not knowing what to do or where I was going. That's when God stepped in. I couldn't believe my eyes! There, in this little back street, was my favourite auntie's little yellow sports car. She lived far from there and very rarely visited this town. I felt totally saved and filled with joy.

I was allowed to return to my old school, but it was now halfway through grade seven. The pain of watching someone else be in my vice captaincy role was at times, too much to bear. I had lost my best friend and felt like I'd been cut adrift and didn't belong at that school either. I was like a fish out of water and to top it all off, I despised my mother from that point on. Little did I know, this was just the start of Satan's plan to destroy my life and our family.

For the next few years, my parents placed me in a very rough public school. Carrying a spirit of rejection, being overweight, having braces on my teeth and suffering with severe acne, I was not a pretty picture at all. I started comparing myself to the other girls and I just couldn't live up to their beauty, their tans, or their figures. I loathed myself. This was the era of skinny dipping, topless sun baking and panel vans. If anyone remembers the original movie Puberty Blues, this was exactly how my life looked and it fitted the era perfectly.

I was bullied relentlessly and the only way to really fit in was to submit to peer pressure and do what I knew I shouldn't. I learnt to smoke, drink, wag classes and even steal to fit in. I stole a few times, but on the last time I ever shoplifted, I felt so bad that I stopped immediately. I knew I had the money to pay, as I had a couple of part time jobs at the time. I know now that had been a deep conviction from God that day, as the next time the girls shoplifted, they were caught and taken to the police station. I felt incredibly grateful for doing what was right.

My first love should have been the innocent fairy-tale romance most girls dream about. No such thing existed on the Sunshine Coast where the boys were the focus of every girl's eyes. Just like in the Puberty Blues movie, all the girls I knew were having sex (or said they were) and I was the odd one out. I was deceived into believing that I was the only virgin left in the entire school. Of course, that wasn't the case, but I didn't know that then. It was only when I was older and wiser that I realised it was Satan.

"When he lies, he speaks out of his own character, for he is a liar and the father of lies." (John 8:44 {Parts of})

I was mocked and ridiculed about being a virgin by many of the boys in my class, so much so that it became like a dirty rag. I was convinced I just had to get rid of it at any cost, even though my mother had told me I was to keep my virginity until I got married. Unfortunately, she forgot to explain why I shouldn't do it, leaving me to feel it was a ploy to stop me having a boyfriend. Eventually, I just gave it away to stop the teasing, thinking now I would finally fit in with all the other girls in my group, and the boys would stop teasing me. I was so proud to tell my friend group that I'd finally done it, but the response from them was not what I expected at all. They just laughed at me and called me names. My heart sank to an all time low. I wanted to end my life right there and then. To make matters worse, my home life was totally chaotic. With lots of fighting, adultery, and financial pressures, my parents separated once again.

I became too scared to go to school, as the bullying had become debilitating. As the sadness and unacceptance grew, the devil convinced me that no one loved me and that I would be better off to just kill myself. I tried to take my own life on an outdoor swing rope, which every Aussie kid had hanging on a tree in their backyard. I remember telling my dad I was going to kill myself, and in good old Aussie style, he stood watch and said,

"Well hurry up, I don't have all day!"

Mucking It All Up

He watched me put the rope around my neck, but he probably knew I wouldn't hurt myself, as it wasn't a slipknot. I didn't know that, but all I could think of is that he didn't care about me. After a few minutes of waiting and pointing at his watch, he gave up and walked inside. I felt very unloved.

We never had a Bible, also known as the Word of God, in our house, and therefore I never knew its importance. I had no idea that the words in the Bible are spiritual weapons that are used against Satan to receive victorious outcomes.

I also didn't know how much God loved me and treasured me, along with how to live the right way in this life. I was oblivious to God's beautiful and caring thoughts towards me and that He had scheduled every day of my life before I could even breathe.

> **"You know when I sit and when I stand. Every moment you know where I am. You both precede me and follow me and place a hand of blessing on my head. You know what I'm about to say before I even say it. You made all the delicate, inner parts of my body, and knit them together in my mother's womb. You were there while I was being formed in utter seclusion. You saw me before I was even born and scheduled every day of my life before I could even breathe. You are thinking about me constantly. I can't even count how many times a day your thoughts turn towards me. And when I waken in the morning, you're still thinking of me."**
> (Psalm 139 {Parts of})

When the market collapsed, my dad lost his business and our house. He started working in the local hotel as a bouncer. My sister joined the wild side of life after experiencing trauma herself and I joined her in this new culture of drinking and partying, as we had the same group of friends. Wet t-shirt competitions and boobs out became a normal sight back then. With the famous 80s music and the rock and roll music blaring, a brand-new evil pathway opened, and I was still only sixteen years old.

Around this time, there were some beautiful born-again Christians in Coolum Beach coming around and trying to tell us about Jesus. I remember my sister Lisa giving her life to Jesus and getting water baptised, but I didn't understand it and wouldn't join them. Lisa was young too and the call of the wild boys and hard partying lifestyle proved too much, and she fell away. As the old saying goes though, 'monkey see, monkey do.' She was a tremendous influence in my life (unbeknown to her) and her destructive behaviour paved the way for me to do whatever I wanted.

All I ever dreamed about was to get married, own a home and have children. I prayed to God like the nuns had taught me and asked God for a dark-haired man with lots of money. Just after that, a young wealthy man came into my life and I remember thinking my prayers have been answered, but I made the fatal mistake of not praying for a good Christian man. After moving to Brisbane to be closer to him, my life became living for the weekend with sex, alcohol, partying, horror movies and rock and roll. Followed shortly after with cheating, heartache, pain, and suffering.

Occasionally, I would visit my sister and some of her 'seedier' acquaintances in places that no 'good' person should really go. The things I witnessed opened my eyes to not just how to have beautiful clothing and jewellery, but also how to get a lot of money to go out and drink with. As my permanent job in an accountant's office was only paying around $130 week, I was living on struggle street. I wanted what they had and tried to make quick money. I had been sun baking topless for years on the beach, so why not get paid for it? I started bunny waitressing and found myself earning more in a few hours than what I would make in nearly a week of my fulltime office job.

Mucking It All Up

Deep down, I knew it was wrong. I drank lots of alcohol and became desensitised to the surrounding evil. I worked in the roughest toughest bikie clubs, football clubs, and a few bucks' parties. I was subjected to pornography, strippers, and the constant temptation to prostitute myself. But in all that seedy underworld, I would hear the still small voice of God talking to me and saying ever so lovingly,

"Don't do that."

I decided in my heart, never to do anything beyond waitressing. My waitressing career was short-lived, but it was enough to defile me and degrade my confidence. Years later, looking back, I couldn't believe that my loving heavenly Father was with me in those dark and evil clubs.

My relationship with my boyfriend was on again, off again, and in those times we were apart, we both committed adultery. On one occasion, I was drugged and date raped. Was it any wonder that this era of sexual promiscuity and criminal acts left me with fear and trust issues?

As if that wasn't bad enough, I was about to make the biggest mistake of my life. What I am about to say caused me so much pain and grief, and I really didn't want to divulge such personal information, but if it can help even one person save one precious child, it will be worth it.

I was in a horrible relationship, and it was just going from bad to worse. It was at this time that I found myself pregnant. Not knowing what to do, I went to the closest woman I trusted to give me advice. Unfortunately though, her advice was to have an abortion. I didn't tell anybody else, so I had no one else to advise, support or encourage me to go through with the pregnancy.

The abortion clinic advised me that 'it' was just a few cells and wasn't a baby yet. I was grossly mis-informed. I wasn't aware that this was a pitch they used, and still use to this day, all over the world to make big money. We didn't have the internet, computers, or mobile phones back then, so I couldn't see exactly what was going on inside my body. I just had to take the lady's word that it was just a few cells. Little did I know that the consequences, both spiritually and physically, would cost me dearly for the rest of my life. Immediately, my body and spirit went into a deep grieving and depression, which stayed with me for decades.

I strongly encourage anyone who knows someone who is pregnant and is considering this option, to please talk with them. You might be the one person that gets to speak into their situation, to help stop them from making the biggest mistake of their lives. Not only by saving their baby's life but also their own, and helping them avoid the physical consequences of depression, guilt and shame that can last their entire lives. All it would have taken was for just one person to encourage me to keep my baby, and I would have an adult child with me today.

Not long after this occurred, my boyfriend at the time held a rifle in my face and stated that if he couldn't have me, nobody would. I was so broken that I just said do it. I wanted to die. Depression was racking my mind and body and my life was a train wreck. I didn't know that I had now committed every deadly sin ever known to man and broken every heavenly commandment God had put in place for us. I had sent myself directly into the dark and horrific pit of hell. Unfortunately, that's where I remained for many years to follow.

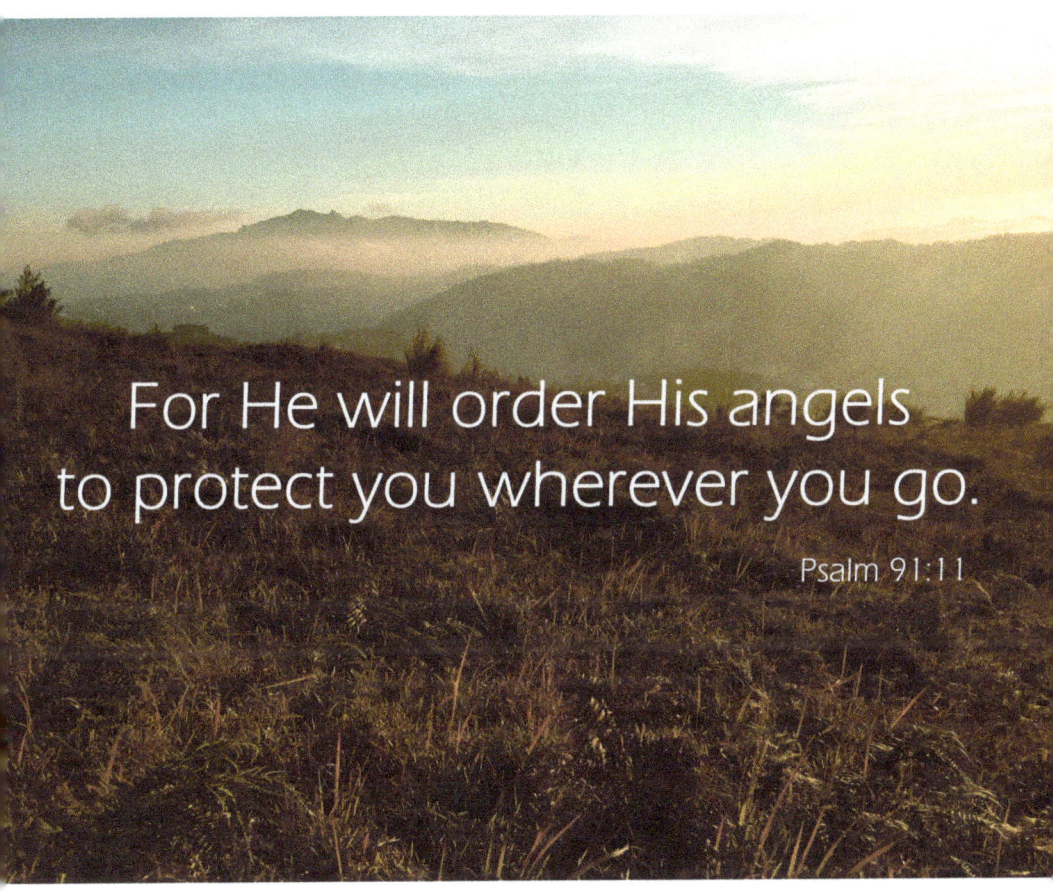

Trust in the Lord with all your heart and do not lean on your own understanding. In all your ways acknowledge Him, and He shall direct your paths.

Proverbs 3:5-6
SIMPLIFIED KJV

CHAPTER 2

The Exorcism

My troubled relationship ended, and life went on. I was still unaware that I needed God's guidance in my life. I turned to what I thought was the next best thing - fortune telling, star signs and tarot cards. Little did I know God forbids us to do such things which He calls 'divination' in the Bible.

> **"Let no one be found among you who sacrifices their son or daughter in the fire, who practices divination or sorcery, interprets omens, engages in witchcraft, or casts spells or who is a medium or spiritualist or who consults the dead. Anyone who does these things is detestable to the Lord."** (Deuteronomy 18:10-12{Parts of})

After watching the movie, the Exorcist, evil really started manifesting in my life in a big way. Most of my life, I had always been able to pick up on things before they happened. One night, I visited my sister at her work. It was an all-women nightclub in Brisbane, where she introduced me to some of her friends. One woman really stood out,

The Victory Crown

a large particularly masculine woman. I sensed a great evilness about her that I couldn't explain.

At some stage, my sister visited me at my unit with some friends, and this woman was amongst them. When I saw her again, I could see an evilness radiate from her body and it was like looking into the eyes of the devil. When she drove off, I told my sister to *never* bring her around to my place ever again, as she was just pure evil.

Less than a couple of months later, I was watching the television and saw that this person, along with 3 other women, had been arrested and charged with the horrific satanic murder of a mature aged man. She is now known as the Lesbian Vampire killer of Brisbane. This really made me sit up and take note of how much REAL evil was going on around us all day every day, and I wondered how had I known she was so evil?

After a few failed relationships, I finally met an honourable man and got married. Both before my wedding day and again on my wedding day, I heard a loud voice clearly say to me,

"Don't do this."

This occurred several times that morning. I remember saying that I must do this as I would let everyone down. But still the voice said not to do it. I didn't listen to what I now know to be God's voice and got married anyway.

Within weeks of my marriage, I went to the doctors for a pregnancy test and whilst waiting for the results, I heard a voice tell me that,

"It will come back negative, but you are actually pregnant."

The doctor came back and said, "You're not pregnant, but I'll take a blood test just in case," and sure enough, the blood test came back positive. Apart from being in awe of being pregnant, I was bewildered by this voice that kept telling me things.

I was pregnant and knew I needed to pray to God for a healthy baby. I was so frightened of being a mother, even though I had always wanted to have a baby. I just kept praying all the way through my pregnancy for the baby to be healthy. I didn't know to pray for many other things.

So many unusual things were happening. One day when I was driving up the coast to see my parents, I heard this voice telling me that there were road works completed ahead. I even said to myself that there was no way they could be finished, but sure enough, when I got to that area they were completed. I was astounded, as I thought for sure they wouldn't be.

I kept having experiences that were unexplainable. During the day and late at night, I started sensing somebody was with me. At the time I thought it was a ghost, with all the talking and other strange things that were happening. A photo was taken around that time which clearly showed a thick cloud hovering beside me. Looking back now as a Christian, I like to think it was a manifestation of God's Holy Spirit.

> **"And the Lord said to Moses, 'I will come to you in a thick cloud, so that the people will hear me speaking with you and will believe you from now on.'"**
> (Exodus 19:9)

The Victory Crown

Just before I was due to deliver my child, I prayed to God that I would be upgraded to a private room in the hospital and sure enough, it happened! I was upgraded for FREE, and I now had a beautiful baby boy named Jackson.

From that time on, every time I looked at my beautiful son's smiley face, I marvelled at the love I felt for him and the intense bond we shared. But always lurking at the back of my mind was the knowledge of what I'd done several years earlier with my first child. I feared it was forever going to haunt me. No amount of tears could undo the horrendous sin I had committed, and my spirit knew it.

Early one morning, I woke up to my very excited sister on the phone advising me she had just won a trip for two people, all expenses paid to America. I had always longed to go to America, and it was just one of those things I needed to do in my life. Normally my mum would be the first cab off the rank, but as Lisa was not on good terms with her back then, she rang me first. That was a miracle. Knowing the enormity of it, I made her promise that she would take me over with her and in good old Aussie defiance, Lisa whole heartedly agreed with,

"Sure! she's out, you're in!"

My dream of seeing America had finally come true, but it wasn't without its struggles. I had a big falling out with my mum about looking after my son, and the pain and hatred in my heart towards her seemed like it would be irreparable.

I went to Los Angeles in California and experienced seven days and seven nights of free travelling, accommodation in the best hotels, Disney Land, Universal Studios, Tijuana Mexico, Venice beach, tours to see the stars homes, limousine rides, restaurants, and a helicopter ride all around LA one night and that's not all! It was incredible, and I didn't have to pay one cent. It was a miracle!

Upon returning from the trip, my marriage had broken down irretrievably, but I was thankful that at least I came out of it with my beautiful son, Jackson.

Shortly after I left my husband, I had a minor operation and that is when I had my first vision into the spirit realm. I had woken very early the day after, as I was still in a lot of pain. I then noticed a round circle of light in the top corner of my bedroom. As it was still darkish, at first I thought I was just dreaming, but when I looked closer, I could see clouds in the light and then people walking around in it. They were mainly standing still, but I could see some move now and again. I knew I wasn't dreaming, so to prove it, I opened my eyes and then shut them again. The people were still there in the light, just standing there watching me! I tried everything to get closer, but to no avail.

The baby started crying and that was it, they were gone. I was in total awe of what I'd seen and couldn't stop thinking about what it was.

I moved back up to the Sunshine Coast to live closer to the beach and my family. I wanted to give my son Jackson a better life, but I was still very broken and wanted to be loved. But I continued to fall for the wrong men.

After moving a couple of times, my sister Lisa, who was born again, prayed for me to get a place in the government housing complex that she was in, and I ended up getting a townhouse right beside her, which was an absolute miracle. People had been on the Department of Housing waiting list for years to get housing, and within approximately 3-4 months of applying for housing, I was approved and living right beside Lisa and her baby son. Her door was literally right beside mine!

After I moved in, I received some bad news. My doctor rang and advised me I had cervical cancer and needed more tests and surgery. My immediate thought was that I was going to die, as I'd known a woman who had died from the same thing. I was devastated. My child was still only very young. I was leaving to go to America again and when I got home eight weeks later, I still had to wait for an operation.

Upon returning, my sister and her Christian friends had started praying earnestly for me to be saved. From the outside, I appeared to have it all together, but on the inside, I was severely messed up. She would often put me on her church's prayer list, unbeknown to me, so I could be healed and saved.

One night I walked into my sister's place and just fell into her arms and wept. I had never done that before, but praise God, she was there to comfort me, just like I had been there for her those many years earlier.

One night she came home from a Christian meeting and told me of an exorcism that occurred after the meeting had finished. Of course,

The Exorcism

my ears pricked up at that word, remembering the movie I'd watched years earlier. She advised me that there was a visiting Minister from America who had performed an exorcism on this young man and there were all sorts of crazy things happening to him. I decided I would go the next night.

Before then, I wouldn't attend church with her. I was totally anti-Christ at that point and whenever I would go into her home, I would tell her to turn that effing Christian music off. Even when she would try to tell me about Jesus, I would tell her to be quiet or I'd leave, as I didn't want to hear that crap. I hated the name of Jesus but didn't even know why.

So, the next night rolled around, and I was off and running to hopefully see a real-life exorcism. I was eager to see the next person to fall victim to this exorcist. I hadn't seen the inside of a Christian church for a very long time, so I thought I'd better dress like a nun. Instead of my short skirts and low-cut tops, I put on the longest nun looking dress I had, which came right up to my neck, and had long sleeves to top it off! I didn't want to look too provocative. I wanted to fit into the image I had of a churchgoer.

Unbeknown even to myself, I had an ulterior motive for going and that was to get healed. I couldn't bear to think of what was going to happen to my three-year-old child if I died. It was too painful even to think about. I also had boyfriend troubles.

I felt an overwhelming heaviness in my heart. I felt as if a heavy boulder was sticking out of my chest where my heart was supposed to be. I was totally broken and couldn't control the sadness and pressure of life. For many years, I always had this empty feeling inside that something was missing in my life, but I didn't know what. Nothing in the world could get rid of it.

I sat right up the back, so as not to be noticed. Secretly, I was hoping for a head turning, projectile vomiting and screaming scenario to play out like I'd seen on the movie The Exorcist. I really didn't know what to expect, but I waited with great anticipation.

Strangely enough, the American preacher was a hilarious guy and had me laughing through the entire message. He was preaching about the power of the blood of Jesus. After praying it over a previous meeting in America, some devil worshippers who'd been hanging out in the car park praying against the meeting, had been slain in the Spirit. They ended up coming inside to find out what the heck had happened and giving their lives to Jesus. I was in awe of what he was saying about the power in the blood of Jesus.

As I was listening to him, I said to God,

"This guy is really funny, but if you are real, I need a new heart."

I needed him to take away the pain and heaviness of the boulder that was my heart, as it was too heavy for me to bear any longer.

Shortly after that, there was an altar call to come down the front to get prayed over. Most Christians might understand that right about now, my sister Lisa was getting a tad excited. The smile that came over her face was something I will always remember when she saw me walk up the front.

With all the fake holiness I could summon up, I made my way down the front and stood right in the middle of the long line along the front of the auditorium. The Minister was working his way across the line from left to right until he got to me. I tried to copy the others by putting my head down and taking a holy pose of hands together, but it didn't fool him at all. He totally skipped me and went to the next person.

I was shocked at this, as he didn't do it to anyone else. I just took the holy stance again in the hope he would finally return. I glanced at my sister, and she had my three-year-old son down the front getting prophesied over. You have to love big born-again sisters!

Finally, he came back over to me and said,

"What are you here for?"

I remember saying to him, "Just girl problems," remembering what the doctor had said to me about cervical cancer. I didn't know how to describe my heart problem, so I said nothing. I remember him prophesying over me that God was moving my house (he couldn't have known that I really was just about to move house) and that God was going to bring new friends into my life.

As he started praying for me, my eyes flickered rapidly, so fast I can't even do it naturally. I felt a pressure come up in my throat and with my eyelids still flickering, I was just trying to breathe as I felt like I was being strangled. As a non-believer, I was trying to rationalise in my mind that it was just me doing it, but it wasn't, and I knew it wasn't me. My eyes continued moving involuntarily and I could hardly breathe.

Suddenly I felt a pressure start rising in my throat, all the while with him still praying for me. Then something came out of my mouth, like a huge gush of wind. I started sobbing uncontrollably. When I stopped, I went up the back and thought to myself, *how embarrassing. Okay, I feel better but it's probably because I've had a cry*. I was trying to justify what had just happened to me. But then, when I breathed in, I still felt the heaviness of the rock inside my chest and thought to myself, *it's not finished yet*.

With that thought, the preacher man said STOP! He stopped everything that was going on up the front and said,

"There's a woman here tonight and even though anybody could relate to this, this woman knows who she is. I feel the Lord is saying 'it's not finished yet!' I'm not going to ask her to come down again, but the Lord is saying to her that it is not finished yet, and He's going to finish it off once and for all tonight."

Well, did that put the wind up me or what, and that's putting it politely.

I knew he was talking to me, as I'd just said those exact words to God. I just wanted to hide, but at that point I huddled in a foetal position on the chair, bracing myself for what was about to happen next. After the Minister covered the place with the blood of Jesus, he started walking around the outside of all the 200 people and said,

"I cast out unforgiveness in the name of Jesus".

The moment he said those words, I felt like somebody behind me had whacked my back with a huge, big stick, which flung my body physically forward in the chair. I looked around quickly to see who was there, but there was nobody. Then the Minister cast out jealousy and the same thing happened again. My back was struck, my body flung forward, and then came the uncontrollable weeping. I had no control over what was happening. He then cast out the spirit of adultery and every other evil spirit he could think of, from pride to shame to guilt. He seemed to go on and on and I soon lost count.

The strikes on my back didn't hurt me, but I felt the force of them until he finally stopped praying. I was so embarrassed and did what any other 'normal' person would do. I quickly high tailed it out of there, swearing I would never return, as I felt I'd made a complete fool of myself.

As I drove home, I couldn't help thinking about what had happened and realised with a shock that something extraordinary had indeed happened to me. I was breathing normally with zero pain in my chest! I tried it again and sure enough, I was breathing normally. I realised that the boulder in my chest was gone, along with all my troubles, and it felt like I had a brand-new heart. For the first time in my life, I could see with a clear mind what I would one day do.

Little did I know that's exactly what God had done. He had given me a brand-new heart. Many years later, I found the scripture that explained what the boulder inside my chest was. It was my spiritual heart and with all the sin in my life, it had hardened up so much, it had become like a boulder.

> **"I am bringing you back again, but not because you deserve it. I will sprinkle you with clean water and you will be clean. Your filth will be washed away, and you will no longer worship idols and I will give you a new heart with new and right desires and I will put this new Spirit in you. I will take out your STONY HEART OF SIN and give you a new, obedient heart. And I will put my Spirit in you, so you will obey my laws and do whatever I command. I will cleanse you of your filthy behaviour, I will give you good crops, I will remember your past sins no more."**
> (Ezekiel 36:24-30)

All I knew was something miraculous had happened to me, and the exorcism I was hoping to see, had been performed on me. I felt free and all my pain and troubles had left.

With this brand-new heart I felt terrific, but unfortunately I didn't know how to change my ways. I knew I'd changed on the inside, but I didn't know how to stop going out and to stop behaving in a way that offended God. One might say I was a bit thick!

Anyway, I didn't know the right way of living and if I did, I wasn't ready at that point to do it. I had been living my own way for too long, but thankfully I had a praying sister and Christian girls in the government housing that were praying me into the Kingdom. Thankfully, they never gave up on me and put me on the prayer

The Victory Crown

chains at their church all the time. Shortly after that event, and after having the much awaited operation, I was told I was very lucky and didn't have cancer after all. But was it really coincidence or did God heal me? I believe He did.

I was now 29, and I was saying to my sister,

"I will never be happy. I'm never going to get my dream of a husband, children and a house with green grass and a white picket fence!"

And she said, "Of course you're never going to have it and it's because of what you're speaking out."

"What do you mean?" I asked.

"That life and death are in the power of the tongue. You're speaking out that you're never going to be happy and that's exactly what you're going to get."

Well with that, I took up the challenge and loudly declared,

"By the time I'm 30 years old, I'm going to be with the man I'm going to spend the rest of my life with, and that man's going to be at my 30th birthday party."

A month prior to my 30th birthday, plans were well under way for a return trip to America. I wanted to go for another six months, leaving straight after my birthday. But at my 30th birthday party, a man I had recently befriended was in attendance. I remembered the declaration I'd made about the guy I was going to spend the rest of my life with, and wondered if this could be that man? Everybody there didn't like him much as he had already been drinking. I was told by a Christian woman at the party that he was evil, full of lust, and to steer clear of him. But still I wondered.

The Exorcism

I fell sick soon after and had to delay my trip to America. The consolation was that during this time, ignoring all the warnings, I got to know my admirer from the party. I fell in love with him, but all too soon the lady's warning proved to be true. He was unfaithful and continued seeing other people.

A short time later, I found myself heartbroken and crying in my motel room, unsure of whether I should still go to America or not. I remember picking up a bible that my sister had given me on my 30th and it really spoke to me. I can't remember exactly what it said now, but it had spoken right into my situation. It both amazed and comforted me, giving me a real peace at that moment. I leaned on the table and, with my head in my hands, simply said,

"Please God, give me a sign whether I should go to America or not."

As I was sitting there asking God to give me a sign, the Christian woman from my party knocked on my door. She had found my motel room and told me she'd come from far away to tell me something. She said she'd been vacuuming when God told her, to go find me and tell me I had to go to America. I couldn't believe how quickly God answered my prayer.

Long story short, I ran away to America in an effort to outrun my heartbreak. However, during that time, I had another profound experience with God and this time I finally got it.

I was now in LA, lying on my bed one night asking God what was going to make me happy. I still didn't know what to do with my life. Even though it was dark, I put my hands up in the air in a diamond shape, just for something to do. Suddenly my hands started glowing, which I now know was me seeing into the spirit realm. With that, I saw a huge hand come through the ceiling and push me into the mattress so firmly that my spirit popped right out of my body. I suddenly saw myself as a beautiful shiny little girl again, just standing there. I then heard a loud voice from heaven say,

"By helping other people, women and child abuse."

I got my answer. I had always hated child abuse in any way, shape, or form, but especially child sexual abuse. Little did I know that was going to play a huge part in my future journey.

Finally, the penny dropped! God might be real, but I still had doubt in me. I decided that on the next Sunday I would pack my stroller and take my son off to church, the closest being a Catholic church. So along I went, again ditching the short mini skirt and opting for my long navy nun dress.

Lo and behold, at the end of the LA church service, they were asking for volunteers who would like to visit children in jail. I was so excited and eagerly went forward and put my name down. But as I walked out, I heard that same familiar voice say that they would not call me. God was right, and I never did get that call. I was gutted, but then thought that maybe it's meant to be in Australia that I'll be helping people. But did they even have child abuse back home? I didn't think so, but of course, I couldn't have been more wrong.

Chapter 3

It's Raining Favour

When I returned to Australia, the first thing I saw when I walked in the front door was the local newspaper on the table. On the front page was a little boy that was horrifically abused and kept in a box at a local caravan park. I couldn't believe it. I kept asking God,

"What do you want me to do? Where do I start?"

But I got no answer, so I waited. I badly wanted to help children who were sexually and physically abused, but I didn't know where to start.

Meanwhile, it took less than a day before my wayward ex (from my 30th party) was back on the scene, wanting to take me out. We gave it another go, but it was still a rocky road, as we were both carrying lots of baggage from our past relationships. His past girlfriend continued to plague our relationship, but I refused to give up and we stayed together. I wanted to make it work, as I remembered my 30th birthday goal and believed that this was the man I was going to spend the rest of my life with.

On the work front, I started looking for a job again and when a friend suggested I would do well in real estate, everything changed. I recalled a loud voice telling me six months earlier, "I would become rich through real estate." I had forgotten it in the busy lead up to the American trip.

Seeing as I had always loved to buy and sell houses, I thought, why not! I had spent many days as a young girl driving around with my dad, looking at potential houses and blocks of lands to buy. He would fill me in on the prices and the potential profits to be gained.

As far as I was concerned, I had all the qualifications I needed to become a real estate mogul. I mean let's face it, I'd been a total BOSS at the game of Monopoly in my childhood years, so I believed this fully qualified me to give it a go. But in saying that, you'll be pleased to know that I did study and became a fully qualified Real Estate Agent, ready and eager to start buying and selling in the property market.

I handed in my resume to a few real estate agencies in town, whilst also applying for a job at a car rental agency. When I hadn't heard from anyone in a few days, I prayed and asked God,

"Could I please get a job with good hours, good money and good people to work with?"

Within the hour, I received a call from a local real estate office offering me a traineeship. It offered very little money unless I sold properties, but I felt this was the answer to my prayers. However, before the hour was up, I received another job offer of a full-time position with the car rental agency, which offered a higher amount of pay.

What a dilemma! Reliable big pay each week versus heeding the voice that had spoken to me several months earlier about making money in real estate. I chose to trust in this invisible God who I believed had talked to me months earlier, and happily accepted the traineeship.

It's Raining Favour

Working in the real estate agency turned out to be a dream come true, I loved it! Not only did I have a wonderful boss, but I could also work my own hours. Even though it wasn't much money, I got paid a small retainer each week. I'd also asked God for four sales per month and was thrilled when I got them. With the sales commission added to the small traineeship wage, my life was pretty good for a change - great son, great partner, beautiful house to live in.

But once again, God shook things up for me. Driving home from shopping one day, bearing in mind that I had a boot full of shopping, including frozen and cold stuff, I went past a bus stop where there was a young girl with a baby in her arms and a young teenage boy next to her. It was lightly raining and there was no bus shelter to cover them. I drove past the stop and a couple of streets from my destination, I heard a loud voice say to me,

"Go back and pick them up."

Of course, in good old Aussie banter, I said, "Not a hope."

And just kept driving. Again, I heard the voice, but this time it was louder, say,

"Go back and pick them up."

"No way, not going to happen. I'm not a bus."

By this stage I could see the end of my street. I put my foot down even harder to get there quicker, and that's when I heard a very loud booming voice say,

"GO BACK AND PICK THEM UP!"

It scared the absolute heck out of me and with an,

The Victory Crown

"Ok! Ok! I'll do it!" I turned around and drove back to where they were.

I thought that if they lived close, I'd give them a lift, but if they didn't, I'd just go home. Uncomfortably, I opened the passenger door and asked,

"Where are you going?"

She said, "We're going to Kawana."

As I watched her struggling to hold the baby, with the rain drizzling down on them, I knew in my heart I had to help them.

I told her to hop in and on the way, I asked the mother how old her baby was, and was shocked to find out that he was 4 years old. She herself was 19 and her brother was 13. The girl told me that her son was blind and deaf, couldn't walk or talk, and they had an annual specialist appointment for him that they desperately needed to attend. She advised me they had been waiting for a bus for over an hour, but it hadn't arrived. Miraculously, I got her there a couple of minutes prior to her appointment.

As I drove away, I was filled with this amazing joy and excitement. It blew me away to see how God had helped and cared for this young lady and her baby, and that He might really have spoken to me so directly. I thought I was going crazy until they arrived at their destination on time.

Now God had my attention! The night before this encounter, I'd been praying to God and asking him,

"How can I help people?"

I wanted to help everybody like He'd told me to in America, but I still didn't know where to start. On the way home from that car trip, I heard the same voice say to me,

It's Raining Favour

"That by helping one person, you've made a difference."

I didn't understand how that could be possible. How could I make a difference in her life? I thought maybe if I helped her, she would then help someone else, but twenty years later is when He would reveal what those words would really mean.

I could feel God's favour on me as nearly everything seemed to go right for a change. Unfortunately, unfaithfulness still seemed to be an issue in our relationship, which left me feeling very insecure. I worked on protecting our relationship from all forms of unfaithfulness, no matter what the cost. I became very vigilant against anything that may lead my partner astray, but little did I know this mindset was about to cause me twenty-two years of grief.

Just after that car trip with the young mum, I was driving along one day and thinking how much I really wanted to buy my first home. I didn't realise I was actually talking to God, or that He might just be listening to me! In my mind, I imagined my dream 4-bedroom house with a sea view, 2 bathrooms, and 2 kitchens. I had made enough money to save for a tiny deposit and with the houses being so cheap, I only needed 5% deposit, which was about $7,000.

As I was thinking all this, I also remembered somebody at a previous workplace getting a pay-out of $100,000 for having a car accident. I thought, wouldn't it be great to get a pay-out of $100,000 and not owe any money on your house! I chucked in everything I could think of. First off, I didn't like the car I was driving, so I thought wouldn't it be good if I could bang up my car, get a good pay-out and that it be 100% the other person's fault, and then if I was just a little hurt (nothing too serious though, as I didn't want to see an injury on the outside of my body), I could maybe be awarded $100,000 for my trouble? I'd worked out that it would give us enough to buy a house, with little money owing on it.

Sure enough, within a couple of days, I had a head on collision. I had been on my way to work when a car hit me head on. I wrote my car off and suffered some injuries (but nothing you could see on the outside of my body), and it was totally the other person's fault.

While I waited for my pay out, God answered my prayers about a house. He gave us a 5-bedroom house with sea views, 2 kitchens and 2 bathrooms and a fireplace, on a big block of land. We paid $123,000 for it, which was quite cheap even back then.

It was traumatising and painful going through the accident of course, but I still marvelled and asked God was it really Him? Had He acted on something I had only been thinking about in my head? It seemed too coincidental to me, but either way, I was amazed and so grateful that we had bought our first home together. I was ecstatic!

Knowing that something very miraculous was taking place in my life, I started getting more serious about praying, but the only prayers I knew were the Hail Mary and Our Father prayers that the nuns at the convent had taught me. Every night, I would pray with my son. Thankfully, my sister had been planting seeds in my son, praying over and with him from an early age, and he was very responsive to prayer.

With my pay-out from the car accident imminent, that would mean we would own our own home outright, just like I had asked a couple of years earlier. We would only ever have to work to survive. My dream had come true and I finally had everything I'd imagined. I had my man, my son, my house, and a green backyard. I was now 34 years old.

My father was visiting from Papua New Guinea. He stayed with us for a few weeks and gave me what he thought was wonderful advice that he had gleaned from reading the book Rich Dad, Poor Dad. He talked to us about buying another investment property and made me promise him we would investigate buying one. As I wasn't very business savvy, I kept my promise to him as I'd heard that the book was excellent.

It's Raining Favour

I finally received a pay-out from the accident and ended up with a bit more than $120,000 after all the costs had come out.

Remembering the promise to my dad to look into buying an investment property, the house hunting began. After weeks of searching, I was so overwhelmed that one afternoon I put my head on the table and said to God,

"Please show me a property to buy."

I didn't know any scriptures from the Bible at that stage and I certainly didn't know the one that said,

> **"Keep on asking, and you will be given what you ask for. Keep on looking, and you will find. Keep on knocking, and the door will be opened. For everyone who asks, receives. Everyone who seeks, finds. And the door is opened to everyone who knocks."** (Mathew 7:7-8)

Lo and behold, that's exactly what happened. I received a phone call from my old real estate boss telling me about a property I might be interested in.

It was a 2 x 2-bedroom duplex at Shelly Beach. Another contract had just fallen over and she'd thought of me, so I immediately went to view it, having had a very unusual dream the night before. In the dream, I saw a potholder hanging from the ceiling in the kitchen. It was a big one and I remember thinking, wow I haven't seen one of those for years. So when we arrived and there, right in front of me was a potholder hanging from the ceiling, I just knew it was the place to buy.

After securing a contract on the property, I received reports from the council in relation to trouble with stormwater drainage and flooding. But I felt God had answered my prayer and had shown me this property to buy, so I just went with it. This duplex was the start of a new real estate adventure.

Once we had moved into this new place, I said to God that if He gave me one million dollars that I would give it away and help people in need. I then asked Him if I could make $20,000 and then $30,000 and it would happen. I got bolder, asking Him for $50,000, $70,000 and $100,000 even $250,000 and every time it happened. We made hundreds of thousands of dollars buying and selling real estate and before I knew it, I was totally addicted. Day and night, it was all I thought about. Maybe my good old dad had finally been right about something.

I could just look at a property and see that we could make a fortune. On one particular property, I immediately made $250,000 just by purchasing it. Back then, that was a huge amount.

I felt the favour of God was so strong on me that even when we went to New Zealand for a holiday, we got blessed. On our return trip back to Australia, at the NZ airport, the attendant at the check in counter told us that despite our tickets, there weren't any seats on the plane for us. We were offered a later flight, three first class tickets home, and a full refund of all our tickets. Of course, we accepted that and spent the rest of the evening being spoilt with champagne, hot chocolate, fine food and first-class service. What was even stranger was when I looked at the bottom of my empty cup of hot chocolate, I noticed that the chocolate in the bottom had formed a beautiful, perfect heart. I knew this was just another miracle from God.

Chapter 4

Can I See You God?

With everything falling into place for us, my heart longed for a little girl. I'd been speaking out for years that I was going to have a little blue eyed, blonde-haired, beautiful little girl with a great sense of humour. I was now 34 and was told by the doctor that it may take me many years to fall pregnant because of my medical history and the contraceptive pills I'd been taking for years. But thankfully I fell pregnant straight away.

I was ecstatic! I would go down the beach all the time and swim and pray that God would give me a healthy baby girl if it was good for us. I had a special prayer rock I would sit on and ponder the beauty of the ocean and the blessings in my life. Life was so good! I still didn't know God was real, but I thought He was.

Heavily pregnant, I went to the Sunday flea market, and like always, there was my favourite Auntie Cathy, selling her plants like she'd done for many years. With her was a good friend of hers, that I knew was heavily into Reiki. Not understanding what Reiki was, her friend asked me if I wanted to know the sex of the baby? I immediately said yes, but wondered how on earth she was going to do that? With that, she got me to sit down on a chair, while she removed a long necklace with a pendulum on it, from around her neck. She then held it out over my stomach and asked it to tell us the sex of my baby. To my horror, it started swinging in a circle, slowly at first and then faster and faster. I immediately sensed in my spirit this wasn't right and it was an evil spirit! Inside of me, I frantically prayed to God asking him to please protect my baby, and prayed the Our Father Prayer yet again, as that was still all I knew.

The pendulum came to an abrupt halt! The woman said that was strange and she'd never seen that happen before. So she tried again, and again the pendulum started swinging rapidly, and again I prayed and asked God to protect my baby, saying the Our Father prayer, again it came to an abrupt halt.

As the lady stood there in bewilderment once again, wondering what on earth was going on, she suddenly looked up at me and said,

"You don't want this, do you?"

Awkwardly I replied, "No, sorry I don't."

With that, she hurriedly put her necklace back on and stalked off, leaving me feeling quite perplexed by all I'd just seen and experienced. Yet again, my God had answered me, even in my thoughts. Who was this God who could stop this evil dead in its tracks? I was so thankful to Him for protecting my baby, and more and more intrigued to find out what the heck this was all about!

During my entire pregnancy, we weren't aware of the sex of the baby and couldn't agree on a name. A bit last minute, but finally the big day arrived and I gave birth to a beautiful baby girl. The only problem was that I still didn't know what to call her, but God did. Just a few hours after she was born, I was looking at her beautiful little face and thinking to myself, *what's this baby's name?*, when once again, I heard that same familiar voice say loudly,

"Her name is Sarah."

I had always loved that name ever since I was a teenager. My husband walked in right at that moment and when I told him the name, he also agreed to name her Sarah. Little did I know that within a few short years, I was going to have to draw on that moment in time for strength, in one of the darkest moments of my entire life.

That same evening in the hospital, whilst giving my new baby a bath, I noticed a tiny abnormality. I called for a nurse who told me that my baby had spina bifida. I did not know what spina bifida was, but I knew that it wasn't good. He in turn called another nurse over, who agreed with him. She advised waiting until the morning when the doctors did their rounds and would be able to confirm or dispel the diagnosis. All I could do was wait! But that was easier said than done.

There was limited access to the internet so I couldn't find out anything about spina bifida. I couldn't sleep a wink that night, worrying and wondering how this could even be possible. Also, why didn't the nurse in the delivery room pick up on it when she was first born? The next morning when the doctors came around, they checked Sarah and agreed that it did appear to be spina bifida, but said they were going to have to take an ultrasound to be sure. Thankfully, it came back that she was ok and they advised me she had missed having spina bifida by a tiny fraction. Thank You God!

Years later, when I finally met God face to face, He advised me He had heard me when I was praying on my prayer rock for a healthy baby and had healed her. The imprint of this miracle was left on her body, just to show me He had answered my prayers.

A few months after her birth, an insurance man contacted us about life insurance. We got onto the topic of God, and I was so impressed by his love for his own family that I wanted to know more. He asked me if I'd like to talk with someone further about God and I was happy to. So a few days later, a couple of lovely young men came around to see me. After talking for a while, I realised that I didn't have a clue about anything to do with God. They asked me,

"Do you know who God, Jesus and the Holy Spirit are?"

I was completely dumbfounded, but I took a wild stab at it and said,

"Aren't they all one and same person?"

They agreed, but explained that they were all different individuals as well. I was like,

"I don't think so!"

But they were adamant there were three of them.

On the work front, I was praying to God more and more, and I was extremely grateful for all the real estate blessings we were receiving. We would purchase a property, move in and do some minor renovations then sell it and move on. It was very profitable at the time, and the best part was that it was all tax free.

Everything was going great for us until one day we received some bad advice. A family friend advised us to get a low documentation loan which had worked for him. We tried it out, but what we thought were bank loans that were helping us were, in fact, one of our biggest downfalls in our real estate career.

Jesus Was Here

Around that time, I was watching a television program on archaeology when an archaeologist stated that when Jesus was here on earth, He would have lived in, or at least visited the place where the show was being filmed. I was shocked to the core! You could say it was my first genuine revelation about Jesus Christ. I cried out loud,

"What the heck? Jesus really was here on earth!" It had finally sunk in that He had been a *real* person here on earth and there was proof!

Before that moment, He was just a fairy-tale to me.

From that second on, I was on a journey to find out who this Jesus was. I asked my husband whether he would go on this journey with me to find out about Jesus. I wanted to be on this journey together, but it didn't quite happen for him.

Jesus First Sighting

Just after that, I was watching television when I saw Jesus walk up to me and then slowly walk away. I remember thinking, what the heck was that? My brain couldn't even comprehend what I was seeing. All I can say is that I somehow knew it was Jesus. This propelled me to find out even more about Him, as I still didn't know that He was truly real.

The buying and selling of real estate continued, and I was making hundreds of thousands of dollars. We had little cash on us, but we did have properties. We purchased a beautiful motorhome and had a few houses, all near the beach. I finally thought we had made it.

Can I See You, God?

I don't know where the idea came from, but I just got it in my head one day that I wanted to see this God that was helping me so much. By this stage, I was pretty sure He was real, but I still had my doubts. Not knowing anything about God, I just spoke out loud,

"Can I see you, God?"

Suddenly, a feeling came over me and I knew one hundred percent that I was going to see Him. I even started telling everybody that I was going to see God. That was until I told my mother and she jokingly said,

"Don't be silly. God won't show Himself to you."

With doubts now at the forefront of my mind, I thought, that'd be right, what was I thinking? But thankfully, my mother was wrong.

Invitation

I miraculously found an invitation on my kitchen bench to a Christian ladies connect group. I spoke to my friend who lived in the house behind me, and she advised me it was hers, but she had absolutely no idea how it got in my house. She was gobsmacked.

We ended up going together to this little connect group where there were several other women who all loved God. The actual bible study itself was followed by a lovely time of morning tea and fellowship. One lady asked,

"Do you believe in God?"

"I believe 80%, but there's about 20% of doubt still there. I really don't want to doubt that He is real anymore, but I don't know how."

"Would you like to take that doubt away?" She asked.

"Of course." I said. "I want the doubt to be gone for good."

"Do you want to give your heart to the Lord?" She asked.

"Yes." I said.

They all got very excited then, but I did not know why. They took me to the middle of the room, where they laid hands on me and started praying. I recited the sinner's prayer, which invites Jesus into your life (I will share this at the end of the book).

I returned home but I couldn't help wondering if and when the doubt was going to return. To my amazement and joy, when it didn't return, I realised that I now had a full understanding that God was real. I truly had been blind but now I could see.

> **"Satan, who is the god of this world, has blinded the minds of those who don't believe. They are unable to see the glorious light of the good news. They don't understand this message about the glory of Christ, who is the image of God."** (2 Corinthians 4:4)

I finally understood that God was real, and everything seemed to open up to me. I knew beyond a shadow of a doubt that God was real. It was like I could see for the very first time and I was in total awe. God was real!

With that, I saw a huge hand reach down from the sky and pull me out of a huge, gaping black pit that was in the ground. I knew at that very moment that God was pulling me out of the pit of hell. This shocked me beyond anything I could ever have imagined. Hell actually existed and I had been in there. I was horrified, but eternally grateful at the same time, for God had rescued me from the pit of hell.

> **"You brought me up from the grave, O Lord. You kept me from falling into the pit of death."** (Psalm 30:3)

I saw myself standing there in what looked like a dirty old pair of overalls, then watched as that body dropped to the ground. Next, I saw a shiny, glowing and sparkly new person step out of that body. It was me and I was brand new again!

I knew I had been Born Again.

> **"Jesus replied, 'I tell you the truth, no one can see the kingdom of God unless they are born again.'"**
> (John 3:3)

In that moment, God spoke to me clearly, and I finally knew one hundred percent that the loud voice that had been guiding and directing me for so long… was God himself! The creator of the universe, creator of ALL things! He said,

"Everything that you've ever done wrong in that body, stays with that body that's crumpled up on the ground. That is the old Joanne, and everything you ever did is now dead and is left behind. You are now a new creation in Christ."

> **"This means that anyone who belongs to Christ has become a new person. The old life is gone; a new life has begun."** (2 Corinthians 5:17)

With that full revelation that I wasn't going to hell and that I had just had all my sins wiped away from me forever, I was filled with joy overflowing, and an exhilaration that I still have to this very day. I felt like I was bouncing off the walls!

I couldn't believe that one, God was real; and two, hell was real; and neither were fairy tales. My head was spinning, and my heart was filled with such love and extreme gratefulness to God. I couldn't believe that He had never given up on me and that He was so loving, and kind enough to forgive me for all my wicked sins.

To see that black pit in the ground and me being pulled out of it, still sends shivers down my spine. To know that hell was where I would have gone if I had died prior to that day, I am eternally grateful for that alone.

I tried to tell everybody what had happened to me, and that God was real and not just a fairy tale. I rang everyone, but nobody would listen. I was horrified! Why won't anyone believe me? I'm trying to save them, but they refused to believe. They couldn't believe. They were just like I was for the first thirty-five years. Satan had blinded me just as he was still blinding them. But the joy inside me couldn't stop me from shouting God's name and telling anyone I could that Jesus was real. I was shown the truth, and the truth had set me free.

A Little Change is a Good Thing

Before I was saved, I had been struggling with swearing and would say the F word and many other disgusting obscenities several times a day. I had desperately wanted to stop, but I just couldn't do it. Within twenty-four hours of being saved, I said the F word again, but this time it was so defiling and sounded like a foreign language to me. From that day forward, I have hardly spoken it at all. That's not to say it hasn't slipped out over the years, but I try never to swear.

Speaking in Tongues

I went to the church the following Sunday, and I saw the ladies all talking in tongues. I'd seen it many years earlier, but I didn't believe it was a real thing that happened. This time I asked a lady,

The Victory Crown

"What is that?"

"It's a gift given to you by God and all you have to do is ask him for it and He'll give it to you. It's the baptism of the Holy Spirit and fire. When you speak in tongues, the devil can't understand it and the Holy Spirit is helping set up your future."

Needless to say, I wanted that more than anything in the world and went straight to work on asking God for it. Why would someone not want a gift from the creator of the entire universe? I wanted absolutely anything and everything He was prepared to give me.

"Just keep asking until you receive it."

That's exactly what I did. Every single day and every single night, I didn't stop asking for the gift of speaking in tongues. I added Our Father and Hail Mary prayers for good measure.

On the seventh day, God spoke to me and said,

"Fast."

I had never fasted before in my entire life. I thought I would just have fruit and vegetables and God said,

"No."

Then I said, "I'll just drink juice and coffee."

"No." The same answer came again.

"Just water?" I asked.

And God said, "Yes, just water."

So that's exactly what I did. I only drank water. I was also led to pray for my friend and her family's situation on that day as well. At 3pm, I had really started feeling sick. I was still feeding my baby, so I laid down for a sleep. While I was resting, I felt this warm feeling slowly wash over me from my head to my toes. I had heard the ladies talk about an anointing oil from God and thought to myself, I would swear that I was being anointed right now with warm oil.

When I woke up an hour later, I remembered my prayers for my friend. As I started with the Our Father prayer again, an unfamiliar language came out of my mouth. It had finally happened. I had been baptised with the Holy Spirit and the fire from heaven. I had finally received the gift of talking in tongues.

> **"I baptise you with water for repentance, but after me comes one who is more powerful than I, whose sandals I am not worthy to carry. He will baptise you with the Holy Spirit and fire."** (Mathew 3:11)

I was ecstatic! I couldn't keep myself from shouting and crying with wonder, joy, and excitement. I was now officially a radically changed, on fire, born again Christian. I was a totally different person, a new creation in Christ. I couldn't believe He still loved me after everything I had done wrong and that He'd never given up on me.

For the first time in my life, I had finally found the missing piece in my heart, the piece that only God can fill. It was the piece I had been so desperately looking and longing for. That empty feeling I had always felt in my heart was now gone and I now felt finally complete.

Chapter 5

Face to Face with Jesus and Satan

"So, if the son sets you free, you will be free indeed."
(John 8:36)

The truth had finally set me free! Free from my dreadful past and all the evil that it entailed. Free from doubting God was real. Now knowing the truth, I decided I was going to see God and speak to Him and that was all there was to it. Nothing else in life seemed to matter. I felt like an entirely different person.

I saw Jesus everywhere, but at first it was always at a distance. I also kept seeing Heaven from a distance, and knowing things about people that I could never have known myself. A woman in the church advised me I was working in the prophetic and I may be a Prophet of God. She advised me of a prophetic conference that was on, so I rushed there with bells on. I was so hungry for God and to find out more about Him. I would drive for hours in the hopes of learning more.

The moment I walked into the huge auditorium, I saw an enormous cloud suspended in the middle of the room and there, standing upon it, was Jesus. I was shocked and bewildered at the size of Him. I really didn't know how I was seeing these things and how it all worked, but I was determined to figure it all out.

During that conference, I was sitting alone beside the lake that was on the grounds, when I saw Jesus again. He was standing in the middle of the lake, walking on the water. He called me to come to Him, but I did not know how to. I thought I could try to physically do it, but I knew I'd look like a right nong getting all wet, which would have been the case. I dipped my toe in to try my luck but of course that wasn't going to happen. It was because He was calling me to walk over to Him in the spirit. As previously stated, I didn't know how to do that, so I just continued to sit at the edge and marvel at his presence.

Read the Bible

I kept being told by friends that I needed to read the Bible, but as I wasn't a big reader, I didn't. I had been given an old-fashioned bible (KJV), with old fashioned words like 'thou' and 'thy' and I lost interest quickly. It also didn't help that I was a bit of a know it all and thought I didn't need to. I finally succumbed and went out and purchased a life application bible. To my delight, it was modern and I could understand the wording. What really got me moving on it was I would hear God give me a scripture in my head. I didn't even know if it was in the bible, but I would hear something like, James 1:3, or Acts 4:12 and sure enough, when I looked it up, it was a direct answer to my problem. I then started reading the Bible in earnest and found I couldn't put it down. I was totally in love with finding out all about God. What I found was quite shocking in so many ways, but the more I read, the more I received a holy reverence and deep love for God.

> **"The fear of the Lord is the beginning of wisdom,
> and knowledge of the Holy One is understanding."**
> (Proverbs 9:10)

By now I realised that my spiritual eyes and ears had finally been opened, and I really could see into God's kingdom, the spirit realm. Meaning of course, everything He allowed me to see. I had no internet or information to go by, so I just had to learn from Him.

He was very gentle at first and would only show me as much as He thought necessary, or more to the point, how much I could cope with. Within a couple of months of my salvation, I had a terrible vision of me breastfeeding my baby, but I was a burnt skeleton! I knew it was demonic, and I told God I never want to see anything bad again, I just want to see all the good things. He was so gracious and allowed that for the next couple of years, but eventually, as we all do, I had to grow up in my faith and that had to change.

Face to Face with Jesus

I was yearning to see Jesus's face up close as whenever I would see Him, it was always at a distance and was like looking through a veil. So, this one night when I saw Him walking among the people in church, I asked Him to come close to me so I could have a good look at His face. He walked right up to me and His face was about fifty centimetres away from mine.

> **"Blessed are the pure in heart, for they shall see God."**
> (Mathew 5:8)

He was not at all what I expected. There was absolutely nothing attractive or special about Him. My actual first thoughts were, *wow the bible was right when it said you were nothing to look at!*

> "My servant grew up before him like a young plant, and like a root out of dry ground. He had no form or majesty to look at him, and no beauty that we should desire him. He was despised and rejected by mankind, a man of suffering, and familiar with pain. Like one from whom people hide their faces, He was despised, and we held him in low esteem." (Isaiah 53:2-3)

He was certainly not a Hollywood movie star and you would never have even imagined that this man was the Saviour of the World. He was very average in appearance and the first thing I said to Him was,

"Now I can understand how they didn't recognise that you were their king. You really look very normal, very average."

He had a large thin nose, black hair and beard, and He wasn't overly tall either. After a few minutes, He turned and started walking away, but I desperately reached out and begged Him not to leave me. He turned around and so lovingly said to me,

"I will never leave you nor forsake you. I am always by your side."

I was in tears and filled with an overwhelming love for Him. I could feel the love He had for me and knew He was telling me the truth. These words were to become an anchor for me.

> "Keep your lives free from the love of money and be content with what you have, because God has said, 'never will I leave you; never will I forsake you.'" (Hebrews 13:5)

Introduction to the Father

My love for Jesus went from strength to strength. Now that I understood what He had done for me on the Cross, I was overwhelmed. One night, I remember talking with Him whilst I was in the shower and I could see Him above me. As I was declaring my love for Him, He gently moved slightly to His right and when He did this, it shocked me to see that there was someone way in the background. It appeared to be a person sitting on a throne, but it was too far away for me to see clearly, so I asked Jesus who it was. He stated casually,

"That's my Father."

I was in total shock and said, "What the heck, there's two of you!"

As I had fallen so in love with Jesus, I had forgotten all about God in that moment. All the love I had for Him overflowed to His Father, Father God. Now I was in love with both of them. I just fell face down, on my knees as I knew I was in the presence of a King, immediately declaring I wasn't worthy.

After that day I started having more encounters with God. One Sunday, whilst the band was worshipping on stage in the church service, out of the corner of my eye I suddenly noticed something large suspended in the middle of the room. It was a beautiful golden throne and someone was on it watching the band. Instinctively, I knew it was God sitting up there as I saw His arm on the side of the throne. I tried everything to get up there and to take a peek, but to no avail. He was just listening to the worship and no matter how hard I tried, I couldn't get up there to see Him.

I saw what I can only describe as two white rivers pouring out from the left and to the right of where He was sitting. When I looked more closely, it wasn't liquid, it was millions of little white doves, overflowing from His throne (white doves represent the Holy spirit). Since that day I have tried to describe the designs on the side of His huge golden throne but unfortunately there are no words on this earth for them.

As I have encounters with Jesus, the Angels and the heavenly realm every day, there are just too many to mention. But I will be writing down some encounters that were particularly powerful and that was and will always remain one of them.

Another day, during the church service, a huge glowing sun-like object showed up right in front of me. When I looked closer, I noticed there was a face in it. It was Jesus' face!

"There He was transfigured before them and his face shone like the sun, and his clothes became as white as light." (Matthew 17:2)

Before I arrived at church that day, I had done something that I thought entitled me to the privilege of being a super Christian and I was very proud of myself. But when He showed up right in front of me, I looked down and all I could see was me wearing a white gown with huge, big mud spots all over it. I was like,

"Yuk! What is that?"

I knew at once what God was showing me. It was all the things I needed to change in my life. I was forgiven for all my past mistakes, but I now needed to change thirty-five years of stinking thinking, and the bad behaviours and evil ways I'd adopted throughout my life till now. I asked Him to clean me up as I didn't want to be dirty anymore. This was not an overnight fix and I knew He had a big job ahead of Him. He certainly knocked a bit of pride out of me that day.

On the home front, I realised it was make or break time with my partner. We both loved each other, but I was nervous about marrying him. It had been a very rocky road so far and he didn't know God yet. His behaviour was often questionable, but we did both love each other very much, so we agreed to get married in the sight of God.

A week before the wedding, I talked to Jesus about this,

"I don't trust my partner to be faithful to me." I said.

"Put your trust in me and I will watch over him in that area. Now I want you to refrain from sex until you are married."

"Why do you want me to do that now as I've been having sex outside of marriage for many years, so why does it matter now?"

He replied, "Because it matters to me and it's for all the times you didn't refrain from sex."

I happily obliged, as for once in my life, I could do at least one thing to obey Him in this intimate area. Many years later, I was to find out that it was also to benefit me. If you can go into a relationship with fidelity, it helps maintain fidelity in your relationship.

Cutting Soul Ties

Some Christian friends advised us about breaking off all soul ties from previous sexual partners before we got married (a soul tie is a spiritual link between two people). A few nights before the wedding, we started breaking off the soul ties as advised. I was told to first speak out,

"With the blood of Jesus, I cover all soul ties between every person I have been sexual with, and I sever them all in the name of Jesus Christ. I ask you to forgive me God and renounce the spirit of adultery off my life."

I did this and when it was my husband's turn, the baby cried and I had to go to the other room. Whilst I was lying down feeding the baby, I started seeing a vision. It was like I was watching a big screen television, but it was not a movie. In it, I could see my husband lying on the bed in our bedroom. The light was on and my husband was lying exactly as I'd left him. However now, Jesus was standing at the end of his bed.

When I realised what was going on, I immediately said to Jesus,

"*WHACK HIM! ZAP HIM!* He still does not believe. Please do something to him, so he knows you're there."

"No, I'm just listening."

"Please reveal yourself to him."

"No, I'm just listening."

I tried desperately to get away from the baby, but no such luck. After a while, the vision left me and I went to sleep, but upon waking the next morning, I asked my husband,

"Did you cut the soul ties last night like we planned?"

That immediately triggered the vision I'd seen. I then calmly asked him,

"Did anything special happen to you last night when you were cutting the soul ties?"

He answered, "No, nothing happened, but I did have a really good sleep."

"Hey, that reminds me! What were you praying for, because when I was in the other room, I saw Jesus standing at the end of your bed listening to everything you were saying. He was standing at the end of your bed and He told me He was just listening to you."

"It's funny you should say that, because what I was asking was for Jesus to please reveal himself to me. I wanted to see Him."

I was in awe, but as Jesus hadn't appeared directly to him, it still wasn't enough proof He was real for my husband.

An End to Buying and Selling Real Estate

We were still buying and selling real estate, making hundreds of thousands of dollars with each transaction. But once I found God, I lost all interest in making money and felt that all I wanted to do now was to serve Him and tell people about Him. A war began inside of me that was tearing me apart.

It was obvious that God had given me a gift at real estate and using it, I could see which properties to buy where we'd make a large profit. One of the last houses I purchased, we made $250,000 just by buying it. All I did was paint inside and put new carpet down. Now I was torn between making money in real estate or focusing on saving people's souls for the kingdom of heaven.

I honoured my promise to God by giving away a lot of money. He had given me so much, I just wanted to give it all back to Him. Not only did we give a few hundred thousand away, but we also helped many people that were financially struggling and even gave away our car. We weren't smart with our money and gave away a bit too much, but at the time I didn't care as I was just totally in love with God, my Saviour.

Pride Comes Before a Fall

A Crown doesn't fit on a Big Head.
Looking back now, I didn't realise I thought I was so special in real estate. Even though we had little cash on hand, we had lots of properties. I didn't think I had much pride, but I was soon to find out I had a truckload! God asked me to do the cleaning of the church and all the offices, but I felt too important to do that type of work. After all, I was a big shot in real estate. But after a big spiritual smack on the bottom from Him, I did as He asked and started cleaning the church building. I found it was good for me, as it helped me to organise my own home and got me back to the grassroots of serving again.

I was singing a worship song in my kitchen one day and then saw God's throne directly outside my window. He was listening to me. He was always at a distance from me, but I was in awe that He was listening to my dreadful singing. He must have special filters in his ears, I thought. My family had told me, especially in my teenage years, that I couldn't hold a tune, even if it was in a bucket, so I'd never sing in front of others. However, the moment I became a Christian, I begged God to help me sing. Boy, oh boy, did He have his work cut out for Him!

I was so eager to know everything in the shortest time possible, as I'd missed out on thirty-five years of teaching already, that I asked God if He could teach me and change me quickly. A tsunami of troubles immediately hit me. I talked with my pastor and told him what I'd asked of God, and he broke up laughing, advising me instead that I ask God to change me gently. I took my pastors advice and after a few months of nothing much happening, I took it to a whole new level. I asked God again for Him to change me, but this time to do it roughly. I didn't care, as I just wanted to be changed quickly for all the years I'd missed out on. Little did I know that what I just asked for was a heavenly fifteen-year boot camp.

It was around this time that I lost interest in buying and selling real estate completely. Things started getting tough financially. We had made a big mistake in a huge real estate venture, and it wasn't looking good. With a turn in the market, we had to sell some properties off because we had over-extended ourselves. I had to fast and pray so much during this time, and just when things would get a bit too much, God would help us out. But it only seemed to fix the problem temporarily.

God had tried to warn us about the big venture we bought into, but instead of doing what He said, confusion set in and where there is confusion, there Satan is. We had taken on something that we really should have steered well clear of. We weren't prepared for the dramatic downturn in the market and were about to suffer huge losses.

Wolves in Sheep's Clothing

Round this time, a woman in leadership deceived us into lending her money to buy her family's first home. This mature woman was well known in Christian leadership at my church, and I trusted her. I couldn't believe she had tricked me and taken advantage of my generosity and naivety in God. Because of this treachery and betrayal, we lost over $200,000, but the resulting pain, suffering and anger lasted many years.

Face to Face with Satan

Oblivious to the mounting trouble that was brewing, I signed up to do a full-time bible college course. By this stage, people had told me a bit about Satan, but I didn't really know much about him. I could feel the bad things happening in my life and just knew he had his ugly hand in it. But I would just push through it and always get the victory with God's help.

Once I was saved, I could see how much Satan had ruined my life. He caused so much of the destruction, pain, and suffering I had endured for decades. From the day I was pulled out of hell, I absolutely hated him with a vengeance. I know hate is a strong word, but it totally fits in this case. I knew that Satan's only purpose in life is to steal, kill, and destroy us all. I was determined that he would not do it on my watch, and I was going to save as many people as I could from going to hell.

> **"The thief (Satan) comes only to steal and kill and destroy."** (John 10:10)

One fine sunny day I was doing my housework, when suddenly Satan was standing in my hallway, and I knew immediately who he was. He was all dressed in black, with a hood over his head. When I saw him, I stopped and looked directly at him. His face was only half shown, disappointingly looking a lot like he does in the movies. I immediately took authority over him and told him,

"Get out of my house in the name of Jesus Christ, for me and my house, we will serve the Lord forever! Jesus is king of our house, so you (Satan) have no business being here."

It didn't stop him from showing up again on other occasions though. It was around this time that I noticed terrible things starting to happen.

As a totally 'on fire' Christian, passionately sold out for God, I'd become a danger to Satan. I'd also just completed an Evangelism Explosion youth course and was planning to buy a bus so I could take all the kids in the neighbourhood to church. I believed nothing could stop me now, as I was telling people all about God and trying to save them. But Satan knew there was one way he could stop me dead in my tracks. I personally had already had many battles with him and won. But this time, he upped the ante and targeted my children.

My three-year-old daughter started acting strangely out of character, doing and saying things that made me think that something might have happened to her. As she was with me most of the time, except in the creche at church on a Sunday, I didn't think that it would EVER be possible for anything bad to happen to her. I was an excellent mother and very vigilant in protecting her, however paedophiles are extremely opportunistic, and nobody could ever have predicted what was to come.

Convicted Paedophile

Around that time, I knew I wasn't fully enjoying my children the way I truly wanted to. While at the beach one day, I noticed other families who seemed to be so happy and really enjoying their children, so what was going on with me, what was missing in me? As I was pondering my dilemma, I suddenly saw that I was at the feet of Jesus. I put my head on His feet and asked Him to please help me really enjoy my children, and to set me free from the real estate addiction that had its claws in me. I wanted to truly be able to enjoy my children.

That night my prayer was answered, but certainly not in the way I wanted. God warned me in a dream that something terrifying was about to happen to my daughter. I had a dream that a group of men surrounded me and my little girl. God showed me they were going to sexually abuse her and there was absolutely nothing I could do to stop it from happening. I was totally devastated that I couldn't protect her.

I woke up very early the next morning asking God why I kept thinking my child was getting abused, as she was with me most of the time and, of course, something like that would never happen to my little girl. That very same evening, the truth was revealed, and our lives were never to be the same again. A convicted paedophile who had been visiting the church had abused my 3-year-old daughter.

My whole life came crashing down and nothing mattered anymore except my children. The prayer I'd prayed the day before on the beach got answered, but in the worst possible way. Everything I'd been doing in my life up to that stage now meant nothing. I just wanted to love and care for my children more than anything in the entire world. I was broken and didn't care about making money anymore.

I just wanted to run away and never come back, to smash every window, every glass door, absolutely anything and everything I could lay my hands on. I felt I was going insane! How could this monster be able to get to her? All my life, it was programmed in my brain that you would have to be a terrible mother for your child to be sexually abused, and I swore this would never happen to my child. I had tried to be the best mother I could possibly be, and it had still happened.

My worst nightmare had begun, a nightmare I just couldn't wake up from. I couldn't sleep and couldn't eat, I couldn't sit still, pacing up and down most of the time and all I could do was weep for my tiny daughter. I tried my best not to do it in front of her and my son, so they didn't get more upset than what they already were.

My husband on the other hand, handled it in a completely different way. He became very withdrawn, processing and internalising the pain. To an outsider looking in, it would have looked like he didn't care at all. It completely devastated me, and a deep resentment and dislike developed towards him. In my brain, I thought a father would want to bash the person up or even worse, but my husband, her father, her protector, just kept watching television and shut down, telling me to go to my room and read the Bible.

His actions made no sense to me and just intensified my grief. Nothing made sense anymore and with my husband retreating further and further into his shell, leaving me to deal with everything on my own, my grief intensified. I thought nothing could be worse, but once again, I was proven wrong.

I cried out to God in that moment of utter grief and desolation, asking Him,

"How do I handle this situation like a godly woman?"

"You have to forgive them." He answered.

Wha-WHAT? I had to forgive them? I already felt like someone had split me in half, with all my insides spilling out. But after hearing that I was to forgive these monsters, it felt like my whole body had caught on fire. I was filled with hatred and rage. I wanted to kill the men involved, not forgive them.

At that time, I didn't even know the full extent of the criminal offences that had taken place, but God was gracious and gentle with me, only revealing more facts week by week. All I could do was love my daughter through this, continually praying over her and instilling Godly love into her, day after day, and night after night.

I'd always said if anybody ever touched my child I would kill them, but when you're faced with it, you can't. You have two choices you can make. First, go kill them and go to jail, letting your children and family be without a mother or father, and allowing Satan victory in the situation. Or start pushing through the pain and agony and support your child and family through the most difficult time of their/your life. I was determined I was going to have the victory and with God's help, I chose the second option, as I needed Him more than ever now.

Forgiveness

I knew from doing the prophetic course two years earlier, that the only way to get healing is, when the worst thing imaginable happens, speak out forgiveness over the person, even if you don't mean it at the time. Choosing to do things God's way gives Him permission to then make it drop from the head to the heart. We cannot do that on our own.

So I did as God asked me. Every day I started speaking out that I forgave the perpetrators, calling them by their names. I would then ask God to forgive me as well, even though I felt myself and my baby did nothing to deserve it. I also included something that I knew wasn't right, but said it anyway,

"But of course, you know I don't mean it God."

That's right, I didn't mean one word I was saying. Every time I thought of what they did to my baby girl, it continued to stoke the raging furnace deep within my body. Nevertheless, I continued to say it only out of obedience to God and to keep reminding Him that they were guilty of the crime and not to overlook it. God was so loving and understanding. He understood the pain I was experiencing, but after a few months of me praying that, He gently and lovingly said,

"You can now leave those last few words out of your prayer (but you know I don't mean it) as you are just cancelling out all the good words you're speaking out."

He knew exactly the right time to say drop it and move forward, so I obeyed and followed his direction, though still through floods of tears.

During this horrendous time, I felt God was so close to me, and I had never felt this before.

> **"The Lord hears his people when they call to him for help. He rescues them from all their troubles. The Lord is close to the broken-hearted; He rescues those who are crushed in spirit.**" (Psalm 34:17-18)

He always seemed so far away before, but this was different, and I would hear Him encouraging me every day. I didn't know Him well until this happened, but I believe it was the start of getting to know Him in a totally different way, the start of a more intimate relationship with Him.

My daughter wanted to change her name at that point in time and she was only four, but God reminded me of how He had named her and how He knew her before she could even breathe (as mentioned earlier – to do with significance of her name).

During that terrible time, God led me to many scriptures throughout the bible, namely Isaiah chapter forty onwards. He would talk so much to me through the scriptures, and they were a lifesaver to me. It was another side of God I'd never known before, and I clung ever tighter to Him and the promises He whispered to me through His word.

One day I saw God's hands in the sky, and He was pouring out water from a large urn from heaven. He was pouring water over where we were lying down. I looked up the concordance in the bible and immediately saw,

> "For I will pour out water to quench your thirst and to irrigate your parched fields. And I will pour out my Spirit on your descendants and my blessing on your children. They will thrive like watered grass, like willows on a riverbank." (Isaiah 44:3)

This made me feel better and encouraged me greatly. I clung to that word for years to follow. God had told me right at the beginning of my Christian walk, that I had to speak things out loud when I was praying.

> "The tongue has the power of life and death and those who love it will eat its fruit." (Proverbs 18:21)

Eagles Wings

Even though God was helping me get through this nightmare, I just couldn't stop crying and the pain was too much to bear. One night while out walking, I ended up sitting on the grass and telling God that I couldn't take even one more step, that I was broken inside and wanted to die. Suddenly I saw a huge eagle standing in front of me. I didn't know what it meant, but it was as tall as me and I could see it as clear as a bell. As it lifted its wings up, my arms were connected to it and I knew it was lifting me up too. I was keen to find out what the encounter meant, as I had found that everything I had ever seen in the Spirit, was in the Bible. I consulted the concordance and there it was.

> **"But those who wait on the Lord will find new strength. They will fly high on wings like eagles. They will run and not grow weary. They will walk and not faint."**
> (Isaiah 40:31)

I was in total awe of God's wonder, but the journey to recovery had not even started. There was much more to come out that I hadn't heard yet.

Little Wins are Still Wins

Calling the paedophile from a supervised call in the police station, the officer warned me not to threaten to kill him, as that seemed to be the first response from parents. But one minute into the conversation, I went totally berserk and lost it. In saying that, even though I didn't threaten to kill him like I wanted to, the victory didn't come in me going off on him. The victory, small though it was, came when I did not once say the F word, or any swear word. I still wanted to act godly, even when faced with the perpetrator of the most heinous of all crimes. In that moment, I felt it was a victory, small though it was.

Angry at God

But as the weeks went on, I found out more and more and I just wanted to die. I wanted God to just kill me, as I couldn't bear to hear anything more. Little did I know that the pain of betrayal was going to be stepped up yet another notch.

I had told someone months earlier that I didn't know how anybody could ever get angry at God, and that I would never do that. Wrong! I remember getting so angry with God and telling Him off for not protecting my daughter.

Then within minutes I'd be crying and saying I was so sorry. This repeated day after day until one day He said to me when I was telling Him off,

"Do you ever argue with your dad?"

"Yes, of course I do."

"That's exactly what we're doing right now. You're telling me how you feel, and that's what you call a real relationship as father and daughter. You can say anything to me."

From that moment on, I looked at Him differently. I saw Him as a caring and loving Father.

Satan kept coming around and I would tell him to get out in the name of Jesus, but he'd always come back. One night when I was on my knees and weeping into the carpet, Satan stood right next to me, victoriously looking down at me like he had won the battle. So, I said to him,

"I may be down right now, but I'm going to get back up again and I will have the victory. You are going to be cast into the lake of fire forever. Get out in the mighty name of Jesus Christ!" He left. The pain in my heart was engulfing everything in my life. There was nobody there to support or comfort me, including my husband and family. There were only a couple of close friends that had endured child sexual abuse themselves, but I was totally reliant on God to comfort me. Nobody could help ease the pain that I felt.

To make matters worse, the real estate market slumped, and we needed to offload properties quickly. I couldn't work anymore and didn't care about our properties. Our million-dollar real estate portfolio and assets continued to dwindle.

The prayer I'd cried out to Jesus on the beach that day a few months earlier had come true. All I cared about now were my children being happy, healthy and whole. Every day I would speak wholeness over my daughter, prophesying,

"Jesus has come to give us life and gives it to the full,"

and

"For me and my house we will serve the Lord forever."

I'd continue every day speaking that out, but every week I'd hear more information, until one day I couldn't take it anymore. I just had to seek vengeance for the abuse of my baby girl.

God finally stepped in when I really couldn't take anymore. He promised me I was going to see justice and see it in my lifetime. I'd been crying out to Him, am I ever going to see justice? As I'd been contacting the police every day, every week, and every month, but to no avail.

That morning when I wanted to go out and seek justice on the paedophiles, I saw God's huge hand come down through the ceiling of the house and He was holding a rope. When He pulled the rope back towards heaven, the two paedophiles were hanging dead on it. He was clenching His hand like a fist, and He had a signet ring on His finger. I had never seen this before. I was so broken I didn't even look up the vision in the concordance. I said to God,

"You better tell me what it means as soon as I open the bible otherwise, I'm going out to seek severe vengeance on them."

I opened the bible and there it was on the page. There in writing was His solemn promise in a few different paragraphs,

> "For I am the Lord! What I threaten always happens. There will be no delays, you rebels of Israel! I will fulfil my threat of destruction in your own lifetime, says the Sovereign Lord. "Son of man, the people of Israel are saying, his visons won't come true for a long, long time." Therefore, give them this message from the Sovereign Lord: no more delay! I will now do everything I have threatened! I, the Sovereign Lord, have spoken. I will raise my fist towards all the lying prophets."
> (Ezekiel 12:25-28 & Ezekiel 13:9 {Parts of verses})

He said, "Look in the book of Esther and read about the signet ring," and I found it was incredibly significant. It was the king's personal signature, a symbol of authority used for sealing covenants and sanctioning decrees. When a king sanctioned a decree and sealed it, nothing could change what had been sealed. What He was showing me was that He was going to deal with these guys, but He was not just saying it, He was also sealing it with His own personal signature, and nothing at all could change that decision.

After that, it was surely enough for me to leave it in God's hands, as I trusted Him. But a few days later He reminded me of the men hanging on the rope and He said,

"You missed something, the part about the hangings."

I went back again and reread the book of Esther. Through the situation with Haman being hung on the gallows (he had planned to kill Gods Chosen people, but it backfired, and he was hung himself), that's when God showed me the reason why the paedophiles were getting hung on the rope. They, like Haman, had been planning to end Gods chosen child/my child's life and because of that, it will rebound on them. With that new information, I was ever so grateful that He had saved my daughter's life. It also explained why He supernaturally intervened. (Please see extra miracle to do with this in the next chapter).

Over the next ten years, I would speak out daily, reminding God of his promise.

"I will see justice in my lifetime and the time is now!"

I trusted God, even though I could not see it happening. I thought the time was right then and there, but I found His timing was not our timing.

> **"But you must not forget, dear friends, that a day is like a thousand years to the Lord and a thousand years is like a day."** (2 Peter 3:8)

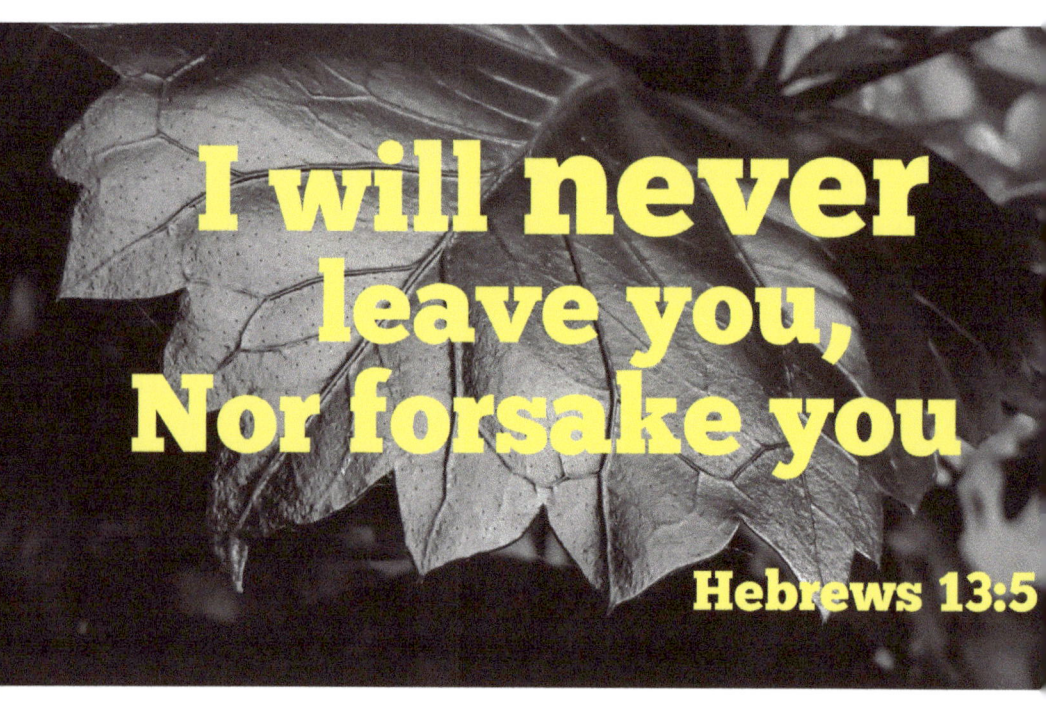

Chapter 6

Be Careful What You Pray For

New Family Members

I had never thought of ever having any more children until one day, several weeks after the crimes against my daughter, God placed it on my heart to have another baby. An excitement filled my heart and a new joy rose inside me. I said to God,

"If it really is you wanting to bless me with another child, please show me in the bible."

When I opened it up, I read,

> "Sing, O childless woman! Break forth into loud and joyful song. For the woman who could bear no children now has more than all the other women, says the Lord. Enlarge your house, build an addition; spread out your

The Victory Crown

home! For you will soon be bursting at the seams. Your descendants will take over other nations and live in their cities." (Isaiah 54:1-3 {Parts of})

I took that as a yes and for the first time in my life, I realised the only way a woman can ever have a baby, is for God to create it.

"You made all the delicate, inner parts of my body, and knit them together in my mother's womb. Thank you for making me so wonderfully complex! It is amazing to think about. Your workmanship is marvellous and how well I know it. You were there while I was being formed in utter seclusion! You saw me before I was born and scheduled each day of my life before I began to breathe. Every day was recorded in your book!"
(Psalm 139:13-16)

So I asked God,

"If it will be good for us, could you please give me a healthy baby girl and let it happen by my birthday?"

The doctor advised me it could take years for me to fall pregnant, as I was nearly forty years old and had been on the pill for a long time. Only weeks later I was told I was pregnant and had received the news by my birthday. I'd call that a miracle!

The doctor asked if I wanted an amniocentesis test done on the baby, as there was an extremely high chance, at my age, that something could be wrong with it. I immediately said no, as even if the test came back that something was wrong, getting rid of the baby could never be an option ever again. If God thought it was good for us to have another baby, that little person He gave us would be perfect no matter what they were like.

Be Careful What You Pray For

Throughout my pregnancy, the police investigations were still ongoing, and to my horror, there was not much they could do to bring about a conviction and justice. Because she was only three years old, it was very hard to prove anything. The pain of what had happened was unbearable and, to make matters worse, our real estate investments were teetering on being lost forever. But God kept talking to me and helping me through each day.

As God had named our first daughter Sarah, I wanted God to tell us the name of our new baby too. After a few months, He gave us the name Gabrielle, which was brilliant as it was neither a boy nor girl's name.

Even as we celebrated the pregnancy, our marriage was buckling under the weight of so many (aforementioned) demonic attacks. Because of that, we had a lot of unforgiveness and resentment towards each other. But I'd resolved in my heart that I'd never break up with him, no matter how hard things got. I had fought so long and so hard just to keep my family together, and never wanted to give Satan the satisfaction of breaking up our family. My husband still hadn't found God and now didn't want anything to do with Christianity, as he'd been so hurt by the church. That drove a huge wedge between us, but I kept going to church every week. With our four-million-dollar financial venture about to be lost forever, I cried out to the Lord,

"I know you're big enough to help us, so please help us before it's too late."

We had potential parties interested in this investment, so it looked like it was not too late to be saved. But as I stood there hanging out the washing one day, I heard GOD speak to me in that same familiar loud voice and say,

"Be careful what you pray for."

The Victory Crown

In that moment, God showed me myself sitting in a car in New Zealand. I had been there a year before, and I was praying and quoting scripture to Him and saying,

"Please God, make me humble. You draw close to the humble but far from the proud."

I truly wanted to be humble, but I had *no idea* what that was going to entail! God then showed me in that moment that I was going to lose absolutely everything.

I screamed, "No not that way, not the money, please, not the money."

He didn't save us and we lost everything. I couldn't believe it, but I had learnt that God only does what is good for us and this *must* have been good for us, even if I couldn't see how. It was yet another devastating blow.

I didn't think I had much pride left at that point, but boy, I was totally deceived, I had heaps. Everything was stripped away from us. I've never been so embarrassed in all my life. We had absolutely nothing left but the shirts on our backs, and for the first time in a long time, we now owed money which could never be repaid.

Satan's voice was constantly whispering in my ear,

"Just slit your wrists and the pain will all be over."

The voice was so clear but I knew exactly who it was, and it certainly wasn't God. I commanded him to leave in Jesus's mighty name and declared how God would restore everything to me:

> **"For I know the plans I have for you, declares the Lord. They are plans for good and not for disaster, to give you a future and a hope. In those days, you will pray, I**

will listen. If you look for me in earnest, you will find me when you seek me. I will be found by you, says the Lord. I will end your captivity and restore your fortunes."
(Jeremiah 29:11-14 {Parts of})

The Miracle of Our New Baby Girl

We finally welcomed a beautiful baby girl into the world, and that new life breathed new life into our whole family. It was miraculous that God was so good to us, giving us a very healthy baby in our older years. But as soon as she was born, Satan tried to steal her identity.

For the whole nine months I was pregnant, we had both agreed that the baby's name would be Gabrielle. But now she was here, my husband tried to change it to Gabriella, and he wouldn't budge. I reminded him of the day when God had given him, not just me, a revelation about her name, but he stubbornly refused. After nearly a week, I just started calling her by her God given name of Gabrielle, which means 'woman of God' and 'God is my strong man!' Faced with this, my husband settled for giving Gabrielle her middle name, Bethany.

Fifteen years later, God brought to my attention Gabrielle's birth date, the 7th of March, and its significance to the Jewish people, God's chosen people. Unbeknown to me, it just so happens the day Gabrielle was born was (is) the date when the Jewish people celebrate the victory of when the Jews overpowered their enemies (Haman's plot to kill Gods chosen people), all because of the decree that was made with the seal of the Kings signet ring.

> "So on the 7th March the two decrees of the king were put into effect. On that day, the enemies of the Jews had hoped to destroy them, but quite the opposite happened. It was the Jews who overpowered their enemies."
> (Esther 9:1)

God of the Little Things

It was excruciatingly painful to be back renting a house, knowing that just months earlier we were millionaires. We were now struggling just to pay the rent and keep food on the table. It was a nightmare, but I quickly realised that the God I had known up till then had been the God of the massive things. A generous, benevolent, and extravagant God who had lavished us with outrageously big blessings. Little did I know that now it was time to meet the God of the little things.

After we lost everything, a lady from our church brought us around beautiful fresh bread each week. It was very humbling, but I was grateful for our daily bread, just like in Our Father's prayer, *give us this day, our daily bread*.

It wasn't long before we were the ones collecting the bread from the bakery and distributing it to the church. My husband found work as a milkman, so we had an abundant amount of milk, cheese, and other dairy products. We were given clothes for the children, and it seemed that every little thing He gave us was so special and helped me to see how deep his love was.

Women's Leader Ripped us off

With money issues still ongoing, I continued to liaise with the women's leader who had stolen our money to buy her house. With the betrayal of this women's leader and her husband, we were left out-of-pocket well over $200,000. I still couldn't understand how a Christian leader and a deacon in the church, could do such a treacherous thing to a new Christian, with no consequences!

It didn't take long before she and all her family up and left the church, after many unsuccessful meetings to settle the matter with the aid of head pastors from three different churches.

Nothing prepared me for the hatred and the anger I felt towards her. It was equivalent to how I felt about the paedophiles. That hatred for both her and the paedophiles began to eat away at me, stoking an unquenchable fire deep within me. Dealing with the paedophiles, the Christian con artist, the loss of all our real estate and finances, coupled with the breakdown of our marriage and the struggle of raising a teenage son and providing for our other small children was just beyond comprehension.

I certainly didn't have enough wisdom at that stage, or knowledge of how to handle these situations that were arising, but I tried to be as godly as possible through all my dealings. The old Joanne wanted to scream and shout and abuse the heck out of them, but God had different plans for me. He wanted me to change and act in a new way, a way that was holy. No swearing, no physical violence, no abusing. He wanted me to completely trust in Him to fix it.

He wanted me to develop the fruits of the Holy Spirit, which are love, joy, peace, patience, kindness, generosity, faithfulness, gentleness, and self-control. It seemed impossible, but I tried my best with His daily help. I held on to the hope that God would get us through, and He would give back everything we had lost. I didn't know how, but I knew somehow He would.

Encounters with the Demonic Realm

One day, I was sitting on the couch talking with a friend when I saw a person out of the corner of my eye walk through our house. A few minutes later, I saw him again walk through my home. I knew it was a demonic spirit, so I ordered him out of my house in the name of Jesus Christ. He exited the door but then headed straight into my teenage son's room as his bedroom was in the garage, outside the front door.

Sure enough, within minutes, my son came in and wanted to sleep inside the house. As I was with a friend at that moment, I left it to the next day to ask my son why he came inside. He advised me he'd seen a strange light floating above his bed and, as he didn't know what it was, had felt to come inside. I told him he wasn't going mad and explained to him what had happened.

Later that day, I requested that God take these horrible demonic encounters away from me. Satan was still showing up now and again and I didn't want to see him, or any other satanic things anymore. But rebukingly, God said,

"WAKE UP Joanne! You must start seeing them. For you are not dealing with flesh and blood here, you are dealing with satanic beings, not in human form."

That finally opened my eyes as to what was really going on and showed me I had to be enlightened, so God could take me to a whole new level. As my favourite preacher, Joyce Meyer always says, 'New levels, new devils!'

> **"For we are not fighting against people made of flesh and blood, but against persons without bodies - the evil rulers of the unseen world, those mighty satanic beings and great evil princes of darkness who rule this world; and against huge numbers of wicked spirits in the spirit world."** (Ephesians 6:12)

Boot Camp

During this time, God was training me to be stronger and wiser, but I didn't know it. All I knew was that it felt like I was in spiritual boot camp, and it was horrible. God was strengthening my spiritual muscles and honing my ability to see into and discern the spiritual realm. Only by allowing me to go through that, would He get the result that was required of me. Boot camp was relentless and lasted for ten more years, but God gave me a word of hope that sustained me through it all. He said,

> **"I am holding you by your right hand, I the Lord your God, and I say to you, do not be afraid. I am here to help you. Despised though you are, O Israel, don't be afraid, for I will help you. I am the Lord your redeemer. I am the Holy One of Israel. You will be a new threshing instrument with many sharp teeth. You will tear all your enemies apart, making chaff of mountains."** (Isaiah 41:13-16)

I was full of self-pity, exuding a real 'woe is me' attitude. I was diagnosed with post-traumatic stress disorder (PTSD) from what had happened to my daughter and because of that, I had trouble letting my children out of my sight. The grieving and crying continued for many years to follow, every situation seeming to trigger me. But throughout all this, the one thing God knew about me was that I am a fighter and when things are unjust, I won't rest till justice is done. I wanted to please God so much that any pain was worth it if I could hear Him or see Him. I just wanted more and more of Him. I didn't run away from Him like everyone thought I would do. I ran to Him even faster than before all the bad stuff happened. I clung to Him as if my life depended on it, and it did.

God's Got a Sense of Humour

During this time, I experienced a side of God I never knew existed, His humorous side. He started doing funny things to make me laugh, usually when I was being extremely serious or cracking a sad. On one occasion, I was chucking the biggest hissy fit on my bed, crying and carrying on worse than a toddler, punching the pillow and not wanting to get out of bed.

"So, what do you say to all that then?" I said, expecting Him to tell me it was okay and that He loved me. But to my surprise, I saw God's hand reach down through the ceiling and put something in my mouth. It was a huge baby's dummy.

I'm like, "what the heck?"

Then I saw His hands reach down and tie something around my waist, and when I looked down, I saw a giant nappy.

I'm like, "What are you doing?"

And with a laugh in His voice He said, "if you're going to act like a baby, I'm going to treat you like one."

I just cracked up laughing, as it really was hilarious. I said to Him,

"I didn't know you were funny."

"Well, where do you think you get your sense of humour from?"

He often joked with me after that, in profoundly serious situations, and especially when I was sulking or upset.

A Warrior is Born

One thing about me is that even though I was down, the warrior side of me was becoming much stronger, and I knew I'd never stop until I saw justice for my daughter.

From the moment I found out that my little girl had been assaulted, I stormed the police station and rang the newspapers and TV channels, in an effort to get these paedophiles put away. I wasn't going down without a fight.

I gathered up every piece of information about the paedophiles that I could. One was a convicted paedophile who was serving a suspended jail sentence in the local community. Even though he was on parole, I found out that he still had a children's blue card, which allowed him to work with small children at an amusement park, all whilst he was on this so called 'strict suspended jail sentence.' This allowed the paedophile access to young children, even while he was being investigated for a new allegation of child abuse! It was infuriating and heart breaking.

I was advised to leak this information to the newspapers, and I also reported it to a child abuse advocacy source which also acted on it. It was to let the public know of the QLD Correctional Services monumental failure to protect children in our communities. All of this ended in Queensland's Correctional Services coming under fire not long after that, with the local newspaper advising it had found that ALL of Queensland's parole services were failing in one way or another. The Maroochydore office was reported as having the most problems anywhere in Queensland.

I petitioned a local member of parliament over and over, but without success. We asked the QLD government to change the laws in relation to child amusement parks, where said parks would strictly be required to only hire staff with a current Child Safety Blue card. Unfortunately, the government did nothing about it back then, and to this day in 2023, they still don't require this protective measure to ensure our children's safety. I will never understand that.

A Legal Miracle

After we had spent the last of our money on a solicitor, trying to recoup the money loaned to the con artist who had ripped us off, we could go no further. Weeping and screaming in rage and grief, I had to let it all go, as I had done so many times before. We'd tried everything possible to get our money back from her, but to no avail. I was in such distress that I couldn't even speak. I locked myself in my bedroom and remain silent for hours (which was a miracle in itself). I yelled out to God that the battle was now His and at that point in time, I could only put all my trust in Him yet again.

> **"No one who trusts in you will ever be disgraced, but disgrace comes to those who try to deceive others."**
> (Psalm 25:3)

Two months after that, my mother sold her unit to help lift the burden from us. I cried out to the Lord for Him to help us as we were completely broke, with nothing in the bank, no home to call our own and owed so much money it hurt to think about it. God heard and God moved! He brought not just one solicitor into our circumstance, but two.

The first was one of the biggest solicitors in Brisbane, who took up our case pro bono (for free) against the woman from church. The second solicitor took on the case of taking the paedophiles to civil court on a no win no pay basis.

Even though the stress of it all took a huge toll on myself and my family, one good thing that came out of it was that I became extremely good at legal paperwork, and it has been a huge blessing to me and others over the years. It even played a part in how I could write this book today.

A Remembrance Day to Remember

The solicitor God gave us did over $150,000 worth of work for us for free. I will be forever grateful to him for that opportunity to receive justice. It took years of heartache and pain, but justice was finally served in court.

The women's leader went to court on the 11th day of the 11th month of the 11th year, and she stood before the judge at 11am, I know this as there was a two-minute silence for our fallen soldiers (this represented when the fighting stopped in World War I). The court order was given on the 11/11/11 at 11.11am. From that day on, whenever the two-minute silence happens, I will always remember how the Lord helped me and gave me the victory over my enemy.

I never received the money back from the woman, the bank took possession of her house and sold it for less than what she paid for it. Even though the money would have been extremely helpful, to get justice and to see God move so powerfully in our situation, was worth far more to me than anything money could buy.

A New Arrival

I had always wanted to have a son with my husband and God placed it on my heart to have another baby. So I asked God,

"If it was good for us, could we please have a healthy baby boy, and could I again please fall pregnant by my birthday?"

Sure enough, at 41 years old, I had another beautiful baby boy. Now there were six of us.

I had never thought I would ever have any more children after my first two, so now finding myself with not one, but two more, was the most beautiful and special thing to come out of these bad situations. I couldn't imagine life without them, and they made my family complete.

> **"And we know that God causes all things to work together for the good of those who love God and are called according to his purpose for them."** (Romans 8:28)

Love in the Hard Times

People were saying to me, they couldn't believe that I was still going to church and trusting God, even after everything that had happened. But I said,

If anyone were to ask me if I would only love God when He is giving me everything, I would say no, that I would still love Him even when everything is stripped away, and nothing is left. My love has never changed at all. In fact, it is during the most challenging times in my life that I have gotten to know Him more intimately than ever before.

Walking By Faith

Even though I loved God unconditionally, it did not mean I enjoyed being poor as a church mouse either. I disliked it immensely, and that's putting it politely. Now stuck with a huckery old car, whenever I drove past the beautiful seaside homes we used to own, I was heartbroken. The shame of losing it all haunted me for many, many years. Not only did I feel like I was a bad steward of money, but I was also a bad example to a non-believer:

"Why didn't your God help you?"

I suppose that was on my lips as well.

"Why didn't you help me God?"

I still couldn't see what He was doing, as I was still going through the fire of purification. I just had to keep trusting and moving forward, having faith that He would provide for us yet again.

Do it Again God

As I was remembering the miracle that had occurred ten years earlier when I received $120,000 and ended up owning my first home, I asked God again for another miracle. This time I asked Him for $500,000. I knew I would need this amount to purchase another home, as house prices had soared. I knew I did not want another car accident, as I was still suffering from the first one. I didn't know how He would do it, but I asked anyway. My husband was now 57 years old, and we had four children to feed, and no employment.

Around that time, we were struggling so much that I asked my husband to request a loan from a family member, but instantly I felt God say,

"Why don't you ask me, I'm your Father?"

I said, "Okay Father, could you please give me some money urgently? I need to pay some bills and at least $1,000."

The next day, I received a phone call from a person who offered to help with our bills. This person did not know our situation and after I tried to say no a few times, I joyfully agreed to accept her help. She said she heard a small voice talk to her about us and our finances. As you can imagine, by now I recognised that voice straight away. Instead of the $1,500 she said she would give us, when the money arrived, there was a miraculous $4,000 in our account. Considering we were a big family, it was such a miracle for us. With the many trials I had been going through, not only with my husband but also raising four children, it really felt like God was rewarding me for persisting and not giving up.

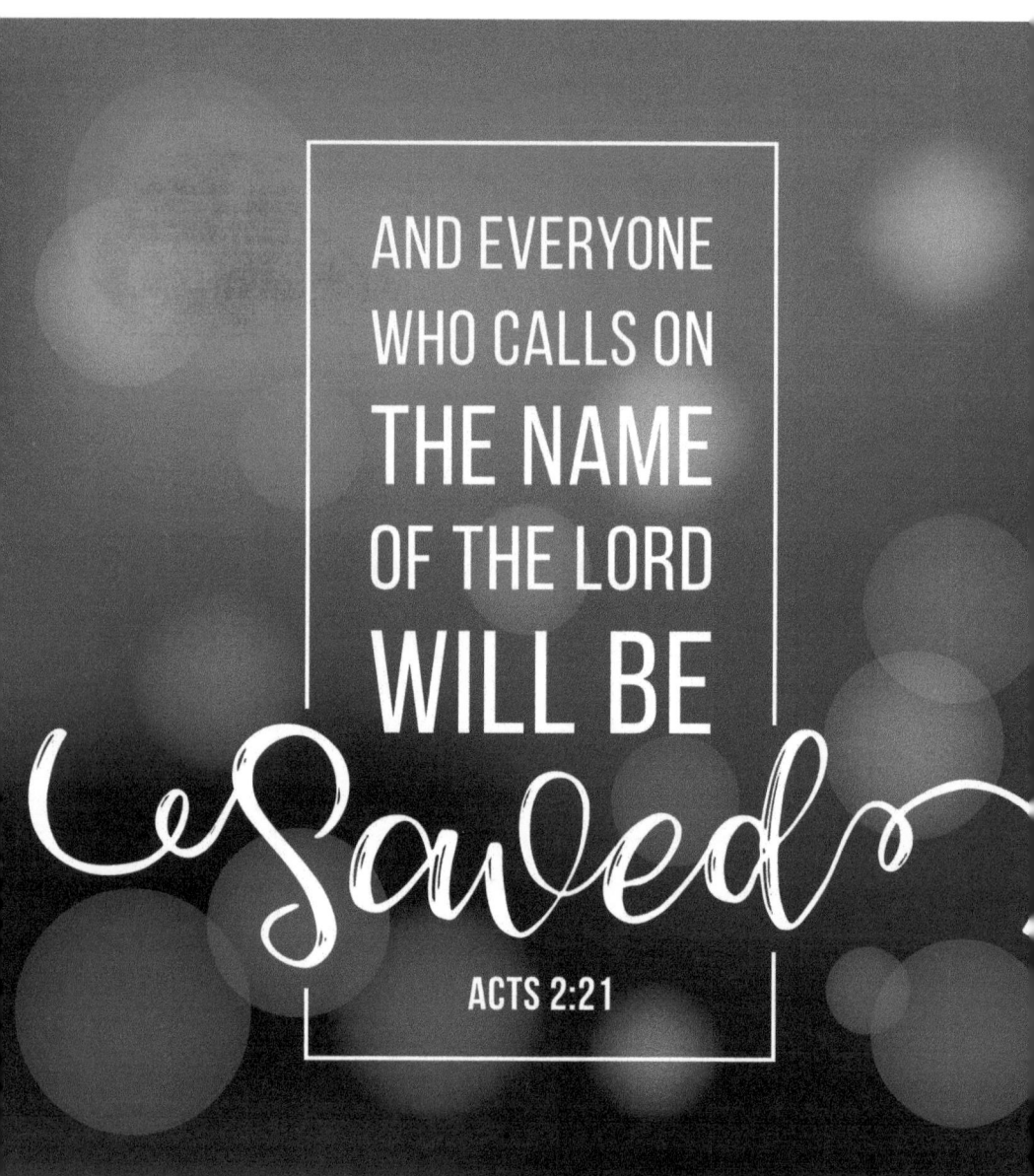

Chapter 7

Seismic Shift

Our marriage remained under extreme stress, and it certainly didn't help that while I had been running to God for help, my husband was doing the complete opposite. He was running to the internet and TV for comfort. This was not good for our marriage, or the family and we were at breaking point.

While on a visit to New Zealand to visit my husband's relatives, the idea of running away and starting again there seemed like a great idea. Even though I knew that no matter where you go, you take all your baggage with you (we had been doing it for years). I chose to ignore all the warning signs and upon our return to Australia, we packed our bags and returned to NZ.

We found a super cheap house to rent for a mere $160 per week, so hopes were high that this would finally allow us to get back on our feet again financially.

Only one thing was wrong now. I didn't feel the same way towards my husband anymore. Before we'd left Australia, I had found out some things that made me lose respect and trust for him.

True to form, Satan chose this time to kick me when I was down and tempted me to near-breaking point. I was put to the test when a trusted male friend started inappropriately talking with me. I stayed with my husband and continued to pray for our marriage.

Talk Before You Walk

For years, we had consulted many counsellors and pastors to discuss our problems, but all to no avail. I knew I needed to talk before I walked, not only with counsellors, but in depth with my husband. So one night I let him know that for the first time in our relationship, I wanted to commit adultery. Only God helped me overcome these feelings with lots of prayer and many tears.

> **"No temptation has overtaken you except what is common to mankind. And God is faithful; He will not let you be tempted beyond what you can bear. But when you are tempted, He will also provide a way out so that you can endure it."** (1 Corinthians 10:13)

We rented a small acreage in New Zealand and we loved it. So once again I called out to God,

"Please give us our own home again."

Once again, we had little to no money, I didn't know how that could ever happen. But as you would have read by now, I'm not one to give up easily. I tried everything humanly possible to find a way for us to buy a house, but everything was stacked against us. The fact we had no deposit and no money for legals certainly didn't help. My husband was also now in his late 50s and he was the primary income earner in the family. It was getting to where we were too old to even get another loan.

Breaking Point

I finally said to God one day,

"That's it! I've had enough! I have tried so hard to do everything right and all I get is pain and suffering. So, if this is what it's like to be a Christian, I'm done. All I've had for 12 years is utter hell and I'm totally over it."

Being married to a man who was a non-Christian was really taking its toll. He just couldn't understand me or my love for an imaginary God he couldn't see. It was slowly tearing us apart, as we were on opposing sides, you might say.

My favourite motto is, *'it's always hardest before a breakthrough'*.

Whenever your situation gets so hard that you can't bear it any longer, hold on! That's when the breakthrough happens. Sometimes you might think that you're at breaking point, but then God stretches you a bit more and a bit more, until you really are at breaking point. That's when God shows up and comes through yet again. God knows exactly how much you can handle, and He won't give you anything you can't bear. That is where I found myself on that fateful day. I really couldn't take anymore and spat the proverbial dummy. There had to be a breakthrough, or I was going to give up on Christianity altogether.

A Home of Our Own

Just after that, I learned something amazing. New Zealand had a special scheme for people like us to apply for a no deposit home loan. We fitted the category for the loan to a tee as my husband was a New Zealander by birth, and we had nothing. It was a lot of hard work, but we ended up getting a twelve-week preapproval for a loan up to

$200,000. It was hard to find a property in the price bracket, as the areas we liked were above $300,000, but at least God had something to work with.

Angels are Real

While we were looking for a place to purchase, I successfully completed a Cleansing Stream course, which was a Christian course to clean you up spiritually. I didn't know I was holding so much unforgiveness in my heart, but thankfully, God is in the business of cleaning up people's lives.

Over the years, I had seen many of God's angels from afar, but until one night at Cleansing Stream, none up close. They appeared like men in long white gowns, each descending on a ladder from heaven. As people were getting prayed for, the angels were standing behind each leader. They weren't close to me as such, but I could see them up the front.

> **"But when they arrived, they looked up and saw that the stone-a very large one-had already been rolled aside. So they entered the tomb, and there on the right sat a young man clothed in a white robe. The women were startled, but the angel said, 'Do not be so surprised. You are looking for Jesus, the Nazarene, who was crucified. He isn't here! He has been raised from the dead! Look, this is where they laid his body.'"** (Mark 16:4-6)

The Cleansing Stream program teaches techniques for getting rid of unwanted baggage and pain in your life, and I got rid of everything that had been hindering me. I had been set free of so much pain and unforgiveness.

But Satan was still there, trying to destroy all the excellent work that God was doing. Even though I wanted to be a better wife and a better mother, Satan was always there to tempt me to fall back into old patterns. One of his favourite things to do was to get my husband involved. I definitely needed my husband saved so the attacks would stop.

New Town

My husband began working as a correctional officer in a prison near a little town in Northland. He suggested moving closer to his work, but I was very hesitant. I'd been advised by several people, who lived in a 'good' suburb, that up North was a dangerous place and a lot of ex-prisoners lived there. Of course, that was the last thing I wanted for my children, as I felt I had already failed to protect them once and never wanted to experience that pain again. Then God spoke to me and said,

"What's the worst thing that could happen?"

"Someone would break into the house and sexually abuse my children."

"And then what?" He said.

"They could probably get killed!"

"And then what?" He said again.

"They'd probably be in heaven with you."

"And then what?"

"They'd be having the most amazing time with you and loving it."

He then said, "Would that be so bad?"

This was God's way of making me face my biggest fear. Since that day, I've been able to use that technique on many other life challenges and come out victorious. So I decided to at least look at what my husband had suggested and see if there was a church in the area. I was to be pleasantly surprised at how lovely the people and the place were.

New Church Family

I found a little church which was totally awesome. It was predominantly Māori, and they were all lovely, down to earth, and welcoming to us. I felt right at home there. Just before I left the church building, a woman came up to me and asked me if I wanted to join them in a house cleansing (praying over a house) and then have lunch with them? I jumped in, boots and all. I found out later that she had thought I was someone else, and I marvelled at how God had organised us to meet that day.

New Season

I went to this house cleansing and by the time I had entered a few rooms, God started showing me things in the house, things that only they knew about. They were all extremely excited and for the first time in a long time, I felt accepted, loved, and understood. When we finished the last room, I felt a spiritual anointing wash over me and I knew I was meant to be there. I also knew that a whole new season had just begun for me, with a season of prosperity to follow.

When I got home, I told my husband everything that had happened, even before he had a chance to get off his motorbike. I was bubbling over with excitement and totally on fire with the Holy Spirit! I had found a church close to where we could afford to buy a new home, and it was also only five minutes from his work.

Seismic Shift

But immediately Satan tried to steal my joy and shut me down. Jerome, our six-year-old, jumped out of the car so that my husband would take him for a ride around the yard on the motorbike. I only noticed he was gone when I heard the bike go roaring off. Absolute fear and horror gripped me to see my son flying up the bitumen street on the back of his father's bike, his little bottom not even touching the seat properly *and* not wearing a helmet! If you are a mother reading this book, needless to say... that's when the argument started.

When life calmed down a bit, I went to work looking for a place to buy. I looked everywhere but couldn't find anything in our price range. But it was okay, I knew I would find the right one eventually as we still had heaps of time. But the government changed their minds, saying they weren't offering the no deposit home loan anymore.

Most banks cancelled all the pre-approvals, but thankfully our Westpac bank did not. They gave us until the 1st of November to settle, otherwise it was finished. Not even one day over, it had to be the 1st or nothing.

That meant we only had five weeks to find a house, get a contract together, acquire a building and pest report and achieve a bank valuation on a property. We looked for weeks but nothing worked out.

With only two weeks left, time was running out. We wondered whether it was going to be possible, as usually the minimum was a thirty day contract. Finally, we found an old house. We were told the owners had lived there for over 60 years and had loved the Lord. You could feel it in the home.

Having five bedrooms and lots of fruit trees everywhere, the kids loved it and so did my husband. We decided to purchase this property, but we now had only five days for finance to be approved, and five days for a building and pest inspection, before the bank loan expired.

The Victory Crown

Every day I drove back and forth from Waipapa to the Kaikohe council, as the NZ government kept requesting information daily. With our finances being extremely low, costly car trips were the last thing we needed. On the sixth day of our contract, we still had not received the final finance approval that we needed from the government.

As there were only 4 days left before the opportunity was lost, time was now of the essence. We just accepted the building and pest report on the dilapidated old house, as we didn't care at that point what it was. It was just going to get us out of the rental pool and back into owning our own home again.

On the ninth day of our contract, with only one more business day to go, the Westpac manager advised me she was sorry to inform me that the department had not confirmed they would lend us the money, and it was now too late for it to go through. Settlement had to be the next day, otherwise it was over.

By five o'clock that same afternoon, I knew it was all over. I couldn't believe it. All that challenging work and now back to the drawing board. I was devastated and didn't understand why God would allow me to do so much work, just to have it ripped out from right underneath me. But even with this devastating blow, I still loved and trusted Him.

That night a strange peace come over me, a peace that I couldn't explain. I did not even cry. I told God that I refused to get upset and that I believed He had something better for us. I had learnt over the years that when God closes a door, something better is waiting for you. But nevertheless, I agonised over all the work I had done, as I had really thought the house was ours. But trusting God more than the bank, I tried looking for a new rental property, but my heart was not in it, so I went to bed.

Seismic Shift

> **"I am leaving you with a gift-peace of mind and heart. And the peace I give isn't like the peace the world gives. So don't be troubled or afraid."** John 14:27

The next day arrived and the date was the 1st of November. A thought crossed my mind that the government hadn't actually said no to the house, they just hadn't got back to us in time. I recalled what the bank manager had said at 5pm the day before,

"Even if they were to come back now, it would be too late."

Still, they had never said no to us getting the finance.

Leaving it in God's hands, I started reading the Bible to get some direction and comfort, when suddenly God spoke to me through the scriptures, and said;

> **"I am bringing you back again but not because you deserve it. I am doing it to protect my Holy name. I will show how holy my great name is. And when I reveal my holiness through you before their very eyes, says the Sovereign Lord, then the nations will know that I am the Lord. For I will gather you up from all the nations and bring you home again to your land. I will cleanse you of your filthy behaviour. I will give you great harvests from your fruit trees and fields, and never again will the surrounding nations be able to scoff at your land for its famines. I am ready to hear Israels prayers for these blessings, and I am ready to grant them their requests."**
> (Ezekiel 36:22-37 {Parts of})

It shocked me as the whole passage of scripture described what was going on in my life at that time, even describing the backyard, which held an orchard of fruit trees. It also resonated with me that I really didn't deserve it, but I could still hope. Within an hour, I received a call that was to rock my world. It was the bank manager saying,

"You're not going to believe this Joanne, but I'm going to chuck a spanner in the works. You got the property. Do you still want the loan?"

I said, "Is that even possible, it's nearly lunchtime?"

"We're certainly going to give it our best shot."

Sure enough, by the end of that day, we were homeowners again. My husband sped home from work and we both just cried with joy. We rushed to the bank and when the staff member came up to greet us and found out my name, she shouted to the other staff members this is Joanne Hayward, and they all started clapping and cheering for us. The bank manager even shed a tear. It was such an amazing miracle and they all knew it. I didn't even have enough money to pay for the fees, as I was short about $250. But thanks to the generosity of my beautiful son Jackson, who so lovingly gave us what we needed, plus a little extra to complete the sale, we now had our home.

"God, why did you leave it right to the very last minute and make us believe we hadn't got the house?"

"I wanted it to be a surprise! If you had got it even a day or two earlier, you would have not experienced that much joy and excitement. Also, I wanted everyone to know that it was me who gave it to you, so they could see my wonderful works."

He was right, nothing could have surprised and delighted us more than what happened that day.

> **"Jesus looked at them intently and said, 'Humanly speaking, it is impossible. But with God everything is possible.'"** (Matthew 19:26)

Chapter 8

Miracles, Signs and Wonders

Finally, our own home again! No more renting, no more worrying about grubby handprints on the wall and no more real estate inspections every twelve weeks. We could do whatever we wanted, as it was now ours to enjoy.

A few days after settlement, I felt God tell me to quit my cleaning job and go work for him full-time. We only had $10 in the bank at that moment, so I said to him,

"You've asked me to work for you full time, so you'd better put some money in my account right now."

Within an hour, I checked my bank balance again and there was $510 dollars in my account. I couldn't believe it, as there was no explanation of where it had come from. I finally worked out from an email that the bank manager had refunded us $500 as a one-off discount on a bank fee. I knew in my heart she was helping us, and I was in absolute awe of God and what He was doing. My excitement was palpable, but I knew there was so much more to come.

Even though our little old house wasn't built by Bob the Builder, one would say it was more likely built by Roger Dodger, but that didn't worry me as I just loved it. It had five bedrooms, which most people referred to as a rabbit warren. The kids absolutely loved all the little rooms everywhere. We had a huge yard with every fruit tree imaginable from plums, peaches, figs, apples, macadamia nuts, feijoas, red and yellow guavas, avocados, mandarins, lemons, grapes, and the list goes on.

The main thing was that God was in the house and most people would feel something special upon entering it. It says in the word "don't despise the day of small beginnings," and this was a small beginning for us, but it was really the start of a new spiritual life I had never known before. I was about to meet God face to face.

Give Us This Day Our Daily Bread

The first several weeks were tight financially, and sometimes we had absolutely no money. One day, with hardly any food in the fridge or any money anywhere, I started panicking about what to do. Suddenly a scripture rose inside of me, **"give us our food for today"** (Matthew 6:11). I realised God was going to supply food for me and my family. I suddenly got extremely excited at the thought of what He was going to do, as He would now supply our needs.

He then spoke to me and said,

"Go get some vegetables from the back garden and cook up the last bit of mince in the fridge. Make yourself a savoury mince."

Miracles, Signs and Wonders

It surprised me to find a remnant of a few vegetables in the overgrowth in the backyard. I then could cook up a savoury mince. The next day, the pastor's daughter Esther came to visit, holding two big bags of frozen meat in her hands. She said,

"Would you like these? They are perfectly ok. We are just making room for a new lot of meat that's getting processed now."

I was so excited! Of course we'd take it! It truly was a miracle, as there were several kilos of meat in the bags.

Esther was to become an extended family member to us, and she would come and stay with us once or twice a week. She worked on her sister's dairy farm and so kindly brought us over milk. One day she brought over a huge jar of my favourite coffee and treats for all of us. She was such a generous person. I felt bad though, as I wanted her stays with us to be a gift to her. Little did she know that she was the gift to us!

After praying to God to supply our food one day, I offered to take an acquaintance over to her place on the farm. When I was there, I noticed how big their house was and got an idea to offer to work (cleaning) for the milk and meat she'd said she was going to give me more of. Upon hearing the suggestion, her family was just as happy as I was. What was to follow was that every week from that day forward, we had a stand-up freezer full of meat, and a milk supply that was coming out our ears, I would also share it with other families. It was truly an answer to prayer, as food and everything else was extremely expensive in NZ.

The kids and I went to church nearly every Sunday, and the people were so kind and beautiful to us. I felt safe and never had a problem with anyone in the town. It was a low economic area, but it was our new home, and the people were lovely. I felt such an anointing on our house and on me to share the good news about God. Every night I would pray angels at every window and door, and all around the borders and the gates, not to mention the whole of the town, country, and world.

Turn the Music Down

One evening my neighbours had a special 20th birthday bash for their son and when they partied, they really partied. The music was extremely loud, way over the top, but that was ok as they were nice ladies and I wanted them to have a good night. The worry was there were heaps of people walking up and down the street and as it was a rough neighbourhood, I was worried about our security, and the deafening music was right next to the children's bedrooms.

I didn't pray against it at all, I just prayed for protection around our property. I prayed the blood of Jesus over our house, and for angels to stand guard at our front gate and all around our fence line. I also prayed for protection of all the little children in the town, along with the people on our street and their properties. I also prayed there would be no fighting, as fights would often break out on the weekends.

Angel Intervention

It was 9pm and the music was absolutely blaring! After seeing a huge warrior angel standing guard at our front gate, I felt heaps better and went about my business. Within several minutes though, the music had been turned right down. That was strange! I wondered if maybe the police had come, but that didn't seem likely as it was far too early. Oh well, I took it as a win and was incredibly happy that my children could now go to sleep.

A couple of weeks later, I was talking to a young lady that was at that party. She was a Christian and had been over at my place several times to attend a prayer group. She said to me,

"Joanne, were you praying on the night of that party next door a couple of weeks ago?"

"Yes, I was."

"Did you pray for the music to stop?"

"I prayed the blood of Jesus over the property, the street and everything else to do with the party around that time, especially that everything would go well and there would be no fighting."

"Around 9pm someone knocked the speaker slightly and after that they couldn't turn the music up loud, no matter how hard they tried. I got really scared as I knew you were praying and God was answering your prayers. The party was then moved away from your street to someone else's house."

Once again, I was in awe of how God answered my prayers and solved my problem.

Working for God

I worked full time for God the best way I knew how and that was to serve. I volunteered in the church, helped the local kids on a Thursday night, and held a teenage girl's connect group. I did whatever I could to help people get saved and into an intimate relationship with God.

A young 11-year-old girl, who identified as a boy, would visit me from time to time. One day, she came over and excitedly asked to come to church with me. She had previously refused to go. She told me,

"God spoke to me! He said, hello daughter, come walk with me in the garden. As we walked in the beautiful garden, He said I want you to listen to Joanne and go to church with her."

We were both so excited and I felt so privileged to hear of such a miracle.

Into the Promised Land

Even before knowing God, I have always been a generous person, and I had seen the blessings because of it.

> **"If you help the poor, you are lending to the Lord, and He will repay you!"** (Proverbs 19:17)

But Satan would try to upset me every day to stop me from helping people. Even the smallest things like wanting to feed the little children some toast. I was told that I couldn't give them anything. But I knew the power of giving and how the only way to ever become prosperous was to give. I continued to give because that was my nature and I refused to stop giving. I had learnt by then, what gives a person the most joy in life is to help other people in need. I had also learnt another good lesson, to use wisdom when doing so.

Working for God involved picking up the local kids and dropping them off at the church on youth nights. Our car was quite old and small inside. As I had to do many trips, I asked God for a bigger car, an 8-seater to help me drive them around. When I approached my husband about applying for a loan to buy a van, he agreed. But it just didn't feel right in my spirit, as I knew we would struggle to repay a car loan.

So, I asked God to give me an eight-seater van so I could do the job He had asked me to do. I heard him say,

"Be satisfied with what you've got."

When I really thought about it, I realised I didn't need a big flashy car. I lived in a small town and my current car was getting me around fine. So, I accepted that and was grateful for what I had.

But of course, only a few weeks later, with all the running around I was doing with the kids for youth, I thought stuff this for a joke, this little car really needs to go. So, I went again to the Lord and asked,

"Could you please give me an 8-seater car and one I don't have to pay any money for, and while you're at it could you please pay off my credit card that was $3,000?"

Of course, I promised him I would never again max out my credit card. But I very quickly amended that by adding that the word ever was too strong a word, but I really would try not to.

Straight after that, I was talking to God about my marriage and begging him to help us once again. I felt a deep sadness at where my marriage was at, as a deep division had come between us.

> **"A kingdom at war with itself will collapse. A home divided against itself is doomed."** (Mark 3:24-25)

I started weeping bitterly. The type of crying that only ever occurred when God was healing me and was up to something.

Within two hours of that prayer, a miracle occurred. A close relative said,

"I want to buy you a car."

I could not believe it! I said no a few times, but her heart wanted to bless us, and there were also benefits in it for herself as well. She said,

"Will $10,000 do it?"

The Victory Crown

I went to work immediately and found the most beautiful eight-seater Honda Elysion on an online auction site. We priced that model online and found it was worth $12,000 to $14,000. Unfortunately, the online auction would finish right in the middle of a church conference that I really wanted to attend. I didn't know what to do, as the price was going up and up. In the end, I chose to honour God and the preacher and went to the conference. I didn't want to be answering the phone in the middle of the service, so I asked my husband what was the final amount he would be prepared to pay for the van? He said $6,000 and of course I hit back that it was a ridiculous amount and that we would probably never get it for that, as it was worth at least $12,000.

He was adamant that he only wanted to pay $6,000 but, in the end, he agreed to pay up to $8,000. Thankfully, I had learnt from past mistakes that I should listen to my husband's advice and I did what he thought best. I put in our top bid of $6,000, never thinking in a million years that they would accept our offer. Meanwhile, I went to church and enjoyed the service.

When I got home, I checked to see what the outcome was. You can imagine my surprise when, to my amazement, I saw we had won the bid. I had finally received my 8-seater van (worth at least $12,000) for a mere $5,850 plus another $1,000 for extras. Not only did we get the most amazing vehicle, but we had enough left over to also pay off our credit card, just like I had asked. It was truly a miracle as the auction company told us they could have sold it ten times over for double the price.

My husband was like a new person, but things still weren't great between us. I felt lonely. I couldn't talk to him about God and the amazing things God was doing with the teenagers that were coming over to our home every week.

I wanted my husband saved, and I would do anything to see that happen. I also wanted to get rid of some pornography images that

Miracles, Signs and Wonders

were etched in my mind from when I was waitressing in my teens. Now and again, they would pop up, and I wanted my mind to be totally cleansed of all unrighteousness. My hunger for God, to see him and hear him, became paramount in my life.

I was so desperate for a breakthrough with God and my husband that I fasted. I told God that I would not eat anymore until my husband was saved, even if the ambulance had to carry me out on a stretcher. I drank whatever I wanted, but I would not eat any food. I was determined, as I had never made it through one day of fasting at that point in time.

Whilst I was waiting for my breakthrough, I received many miracles. I was given a $7,000 brand new bed and acquired a casual job as a pay officer in the local Countdown supermarket. My husband seemed to listen and was understanding more. The teenage girls coming for my home connect group were getting powerfully saved.

On the ninth day without food, a close friend accidentally said something to me that hurt my feelings. I walked into the backyard where all the fruit trees were and started pondering. I felt like Adam and Eve as I heard Satan's voice say,

"Eat some fruit."

I was under my favourite fruit tree, so I picked the fig off and took a bite. Right at that point I heard the devil speak to me again and say,

"Look, nothing has happened. You wasted your time. How can you save people when you can't even save your own husband!"

"You're a liar Satan, get ye behind me!"

Something had changed, but I just couldn't see it.

The Victory Crown

Thankfully, my pastor knew exactly how I felt as he had made mistakes with his own children and Satan had said a similar thing to him, asking how he could ever preach in this town again after the things he had done wrong? The pastor gave me great advice, to just keep doing what God wanted me to do and to leave my husband for God to take care of. It was wonderful advice and kept me going.

The fasting may not have given me what I set out for with my husband's salvation, but I got something much greater than that.

Chapter 9

Face to Face with God

> "As Moses entered the tent, the pillar of cloud would come down and remain at the entrance, and the Lord would speak with Moses. Inside the tent, the Lord would speak to Moses face to face, as a man speaks to his friend." (Exodus 33:9-11 {Parts of})

Face to Face with God

With my fasting over, my prayers to see and speak to God face to face finally occurred. I would always see parts of Him, like a hand, eye, foot or mouth. I only ever saw Him as a whole person from a distance. I hoped to see Him close up like I had with Jesus.

One night I was just sitting in my lounge room, reading my bible and listening to worship songs when suddenly I saw a gigantic angel standing in front of me, he was holding what looked like a huge spear. This was no ordinary angel; it was like a giant warrior. (Just to explain one thing, this physical world cannot contain anything I see in the spirit. They are in the spiritual dimension, where there are no ceilings or boundaries around them.) There was another angel on the other side of the room that looked remarkably similar.

I then saw a golden throne in my hallway with somebody on it. I thought it may be God, but I wasn't sure, as I had never seen Him this close before. As He walked towards me, I realised immediately it was God and I just fell on my knees in reverence. He was all dressed in white and even though He was right in front of me, I couldn't see His face clearly, as it was like there was a veil over it.

All I could do was cry with overwhelming gratitude and gratefulness, as I didn't feel I was good enough to be in His presence. With much happiness, He opened his arms wide and said,

"Come to me."

I ran into His loving arms as I had done on so many other occasions with Jesus. Whenever I was with Jesus, as soon as I was in His presence, I visually would become like a little child again and this was also the case with God. I became His beautiful little girl again, the innocent little girl I was before I grew up and was defiled.

"Then He said, 'I tell you the truth, unless you turn from your sins and become like little children, you will never get into the kingdom of heaven.'" (Matthew 18:3)

After that night, our relationship went to a whole new level. I would get a visit from Him every few days, often with angels on either side of Him and always seated on His throne. At that point in time, I didn't realise I could access Him at will and thought I just had to wait until He magically appeared again, like some genie. I really didn't have a clue how this 'let's see God' thing worked, but I was determined to master it.

It was not even about seeing Him anymore. What my true heart's desire was that I really wanted to know everything about Him. I was still in awe that He was real! To this very day, I am still filled with exhilaration that He exists and to know that one day I am going to spend eternity with Him in paradise. You can also have this promise of eternity, and I will show you how in the chapters ahead.

> **"Jesus answered him, 'truly I tell you, today you will be with me in paradise'"** (Luke 23:43)

God the Father

After this encounter, a new and exciting relationship began between us, Father and daughter. I loved Him with all my heart and all I wanted to do was to serve Him and get to know him more. Before the encounter, I didn't really know the Father side of God as much as I was finding out now, but after meeting Him face to face, it became an 'I love you daddy' relationship. It was hard for me to even say those words. God had to break down many walls inside of me and rectify the mistaken belief systems that I had learnt about Him, what He was really like, and what He expected of me.

Now whenever He would show up, as soon as He would get off his throne, He would open his arms and say,

"Come give me a big cuddle."

"Don't come near me, I'm not worthy! I have been arguing with my husband, I've been yelling at the kids, thinking bad things. I'm just not worthy."

"What are you talking about? I don't remember."

"But I've been doing bad stuff."

"What are you talking about? I don't remember."

"Really? You really do forget, don't you!"

"Yep, as east is to west, I don't remember, so again, come here and give me a big cuddle!"

With His arms wide open and love radiating from Him, He said,

"All I want is your love and affection."

> **"For his mercy toward those who fear and honour him is as great as the height of the heavens above the earth. He has removed our sins as far away from us as the east is from the west. He is like a Father to us, tender and sympathetic to those who reverence him."** (Psalms 103:11-13)

> **"For I will forgive their wickedness and will remember their sins no more."** (Hebrews 8:12)

This was a new side of God I had never known before, a real Father who loved me so much. I didn't realise it before this, but I must have thought He was angry with me all the time. Even though I knew He loved me, I still saw Him as a mean old man, ready to punish me whenever I did something wrong. But it turned out He was the complete opposite! He always made me laugh, even in the most serious of situations. I knew He had a sense of humour, as I explained in my previous encounters with Him. On one encounter with Jesus, He said to me,

"Why so serious? Life's too short to be so serious. Have fun, enjoy what I have given you."

With all the years of trials and tribulations, I had forgotten what it was like to have fun.

Marriage Counselling from Above

Time passed, yet things were still bad in my marriage. I didn't understand how things could deteriorate, especially when I was able to see and speak with God. It just didn't make sense. But as it is written:

> **"Don't team up with those who do not love the Lord, for what do the people of God have in common with the people of sin? How can light live with darkness? And what harmony can there be between Christ and the devil? How can a Christian be a partner with one who doesn't believe?"** (2 Corinthians 6:14-15)

Breaking Point

Our marriage was in turmoil most of the time. I wanted to leave him, but again I talked before I walked. I went to the Pastor's wife, who was a mighty woman of God, and she prayed for me big time! I was sick of weeping and told God I couldn't live like that anymore. As the Pastor's wife prayed, suddenly God showed up on his throne again. He opened His arms wide and, like a loving Father, said,

"Come to me darling."

As I ran to Him, again I became like a little girl, hugging my father and telling Him I couldn't go any further. When I got off the throne, I was running and prancing around like a little lion cub. He had given me the energy I needed to keep going. But all the time this was going on with God, I could still hear the Pastor's wife repeatedly saying, 'keep a clear conscience with God, keep a clear conscience with God.'

> **"Cling tightly to your faith in Christ and always keep your conscience clear, doing what you know is right."** (1 Timothy 1:19)

After praying, I thanked her and headed home, re-energised and ready to fight once more for my marriage. On the way home, I rang my husband and asked him to forgive me for everything I was doing wrong. I told him I'd try to be a better wife, that I loved him and wanted to make it work. He said similar things to me and again, we were both going to try harder. All the way home though, the words 'keep a clear conscience with God' kept playing in my mind.

Clear Conscience

I was in the kitchen the following morning, when my daughter came and asked me, "why is daddy lying down on the floor?"

I knew immediately he was in trouble and called 111. I tried to help him up, but he just fell on the floor convulsing. I could see his breathing was getting slower and slower, as his heart rate fell and I suddenly thought, *he's going to die!* I was sure he was having a heart attack! I didn't know what it meant to have a clear conscience, but as the seconds passed, I was to quickly learn it's true meaning.

> **"Dear friends if our conscience is clear, we can come to God with bold confidence, and we will receive whatever we request because we obey him and do the things that please him."** (1 John 3:21-22)

God showed me everything that had happened the previous day. That in the midst of a bad situation, I had sought out Godly counselling and hadn't left my husband, and I had forgiven him and apologised to him for all my mistakes. I had humbled myself to him, cooking him a lovely meal, and making up as husband and wife. I had left nothing out. Even now, God was showing me what it was like to have a clear conscience. It's funny how God's timing differs from ours. He showed me all this in a split second, but it seemed like hours.

Brought Back to Life

Getting back to my husband, I knew he was dying! I didn't handle the crisis as spiritually as I would have liked. I panicked and rang the ambulance immediately. Whilst on the phone with the emergency officer, I saw my husband take his last breath and completely stop moving. His body went as white as a ghost and with that, I screamed the name "JESUS!" Immediately his body went red and he started breathing again. Though still shaken by the close call, I rejoiced that my husband was still with us.

The ambulance arrived and the officer did tests but found nothing. They then took him off to the hospital and ran more tests, but as it remained a mystery as to what had happened to him, they sent him home. I realised God was showing me what it was like to have a clear conscience. Nothing changed for my husband, and he still couldn't believe that God was real, even after we told him he died. Things still weren't good in our marriage, but I was determined not to give up.

God's Rewards

God could see how much I was trying and rewarded me for my perseverance. I was gifted a trip to Christchurch to attend a Christian conference, which provided a much needed break away. As soon as I walked in the front doors of the first meeting, God walked right up to me. This time He was dressed like and looked exactly like my natural father. I was very emotional as I asked Him why He had dressed like that. Why had He taken on my father's appearance, right down to the white singlet, denim jeans, belt and thongs? He said He wanted me to see His face and this was the closest I would get to see it close up. He then stepped remarkably close to me and as I looked into His face, He smiled a beautiful big smile and said,

"I'm so very happy with you and I wanted you to see the happiness in my face."

Of course, I was a blubbering mess. He then said,

"You know every curve of your father's shoulders, and I just want you to hug me."

As I looked at Him, I could see those familiar tanned big muscles and I felt so much love for God as a Father. When I questioned Him about why He was wearing my dad's exact clothing, He said,

"Everyone is an individual, and I loved those things about him."

"Really? Thongs!"

"Yep, even the thongs."

I soon found out the whole conference was all about the Father, the Father's love and how we are all brothers and sisters. There is only one Father and we are all his children.

Face Glowing

As we were there for several days, a couple of friends noticed something unusual happen to me whilst in the meeting. They didn't know at that point what I was experiencing, as I hadn't shared my encounters with God with anyone yet. But in the evening service He appeared in front of me as my real dad once again, I was standing in the middle of the exceptionally large auditorium, where there were hundreds of people attending. It was pitch black except for the band on the stage. My friends were on one side of the room and it was packed to the brim. One friend noticed me in the middle of the auditorium, and said that when she looked over the crowd, she saw that my entire face was glowing. She even said to her friend,

"Can you see Joanne, and can you see what I'm seeing?"

The other lady looked over, saw me and said,

"Yes, I see her, her face is glowing!"

> **"When Moses came down the mountain carrying the stone tablets inscribed with the terms of the covenant, he wasn't aware that his face glowed because he had spoken to the LORD face to face."** (Exodus 34:29)

They seemed quite shocked at what they'd seen, but I was totally over the moon. It was confirmation I wasn't going mad. He'd been right in front of me, talking with me face to face. I was so encouraged and from that moment on, I continually saw angels surrounding Him on His throne, along with partying and fireworks in Heaven over the conference. It was amazing to see this once again!

Relationship Counselling from God

Do not be deceived. God knows and can see everything in your marriage, especially what goes on behind closed doors, even behind one's back.

> **"The Lord is watching everywhere, keeping his eye on both the evil and the good."** (Proverbs 15:3)

One day at work, I was just typing away when God spoke to me,

"You deserve to be spoken to lovingly and kindly."

He then showed me a man speaking to me lovingly and kindly. I had forgotten what it was like.

"Really? You really want that for me?"

"Of course I do! What would you do if one of your daughters came to you and told you that the things that have been happening in your marriage, were happening in *her* marriage? What would you say to her?"

I knew exactly what I would have wanted to say to her, beginning with 'dump his sorry butt!' but as a Christian I thought we weren't allowed to break up, so I replied,

"I don't really know. Doesn't the Bible say we are not to leave our husbands?"

He replied by showing me a picture of a woman standing with her hand up like a stop sign saying, 'we deserve to be spoken to lovingly and kindly', and it came with such power that it strengthened me just watching it. With that, He showed me that if things continued the way they were, I had permission to leave my husband. As the woman walked away, I knew that woman symbolised me.

When I got home and the anger flared again, I told him exactly what God had shown me and what God had said. The power that came from saying that was like a lightning bolt. A Godly fear set in, and things changed between my husband and myself. But unfortunately, it only lasted a few weeks before returning to the way it was before. Even though I still hoped we could work things out, from then on, I knew that at the very least, I would know what to share with others who were in abusive relationships. I also knew in my heart that I had tried everything to make it work.

Chapter 10

Boundaries Bring Break Through

New Zealand was one of the best experiences of my life, both spiritually and culturally, and I will be forever grateful for the wonderful people that came into my life. However, we decided to move back to Australia.

Upon our return, we purchased a unit and management rights in Caloundra on the beautiful Sunshine Coast in QLD. As I knew that the Bible teaches the power of life and death is in the tongue, I prayed and declared out of my mouth that God would give my husband work immediately in our local area. God gave him full-time employment locally within a week which, as my husband was over 60 years old at the time, we knew was a miracle in itself.

Every day when I made time for God in the morning, there He was ready to give me a kiss on the cheek or speak into my life. I grew closer to Him and encouraged our children to have their own relationships with God, taking them to church with me every week, as I had done for the past 17 years.

Some days God would reveal himself to me as a mighty warrior, a man of war. He also appeared as a mighty Islander chief with tattoos, a huge spear, feathers, and cloak. I also became a mighty warrior, as He'd shown me in the past. I was a commander of a heavenly angel army.

> "The Lord is a warrior- Yes, Jehovah is his name."
> (Exodus 15:3)

Commander of an Army of Angels

I was driving home from church one evening when I saw God riding on a huge black horse in front of my car. Then He showed me myself riding on a horse wearing armour, with thousands of warrior angels behind me. He told me that I was the commander of these angels, and they were waiting for my directions of where to go.

At first, I didn't know how to command them to do anything. But after a long time had passed, I remembered what God had shown me and finally started praying, in Jesus' name, for the angels to go out and help people, to bring down paedophile rings, etc. Amazing things started happening.

> "The truth is, anyone who believes in me (Jesus) will do the same works I have done, and even greater works, because I am going to be with the father. You can ask for anything in my name, and I will do it, because the work of the Son brings glory to the Father. Yes, ask anything in my name, and I will do it!" (John 14:12-14)

Late Answer to Prayer

One day when I was sitting there looking out the window of my new home, I heard God say to me,

"$150,000 wasn't too bad for a trip to the doctors."

"What do you mean?"

"You always thought that by helping one person, you would be making a difference in their life. But what you didn't realise Joanne, is that by being obedient and helping that lady 20 years ago, you had also made a difference in your own life. Look outside your front door," He said.

I looked outside my front door and saw that right outside my new home was the spot where I had the accident twenty years earlier. Now twenty years on, I had a place I had just paid $500,000 for, and God reminded me of the prayer I had prayed when we had lost everything. I prayed for God to give me another house worth $500,000. He then told me what my life would have looked like if I had not obeyed him.

"If you hadn't picked up that woman years earlier, you would never have been to all the places that you've been, never experienced all the wonderful people that you met along the way, and you might still be in the same place, doing the same things."

I knew about sowing and reaping, but this went to a whole new level. When you bless others, you are setting up a blessing for yourself. I hadn't done it to receive anything, but I was in awe of what God was saying, and amazed that He had answered my prayer from ten years earlier.

Tithing Miracle

God really looks at your heart motives. I had not been tithing regularly since we had been back from New Zealand, as we were in the middle of changing churches. I realised my heart attitude was way off about giving to God. When I realised this, I got down on my knees and asked him to forgive me as I hadn't really put much thought towards Him. I realised I had been giving out of duty and not out of love. So the following day I wholeheartedly gave Him my tithes (10% of our income) and did it with immense joy and happiness.

> **"You must each make up your own mind as to how much you should give. Don't give reluctantly or in response to pressure. For God loves the person who gives cheerfully. And God will generously provide all you need. Then you will always have everything you need and plenty left over to share with others."** (2 Corinthians 9:7-8)

The next day, a miracle happened. I had been in a long legal battle that was not a no win, no pay. I was going to have to pay seven years of solicitors' bills and the last time I looked at the bill years earlier, it was around $35,000. I hadn't bothered looking at it after that, until the day came to settle the legal matter. Crunch time came and the outcome was not looking good, so the solicitor suggested two things to me. Firstly, if I kept the case going, he would charge us the full fee, but the second option was if I wanted to discontinue the case, he would wipe the entire bill. Of course, I quickly chose the latter and he wiped the bill completely, even before we got off the phone. I was overwhelmed with gratitude and knew that it was God's way of blessing me and supporting my decision to take legal action in the first place.

> **"Bring all the tithes into the storehouse so there will be enough food in my Temple. If you do,"** says the Lord Almighty, **"I will open the windows of heaven for**

> you. I will pour out a blessing so great you won't have enough room to take it in! Try it! Let me prove to you!"
> (Malachi 3:10)

So why was it I could help everyone else, but could not save my husband? I had tried desperately over the years and then tried doing nothing for a couple of years, but nothing seemed to work. Coming back to Australia seemed like a big mistake and God rebuked me for leaving the teenage girl's group in NZ, as it had grown into a wonderful fellowship group.

In Australia, the problems went to a higher level. Betrayal, fear, and anger were ever present in our home. It felt like I was always in battle, trying to take back any ground the devil was trying to steal. Whether it was with my work, husband or children, I was always on high alert in prayer. I was determined that the devil would not have my marriage or my children.

> **"Pray at all times and on every occasion in the power of the Holy Spirit. Stay alert and be persistent in your prayers for all Christians everywhere."** (Ephesians 6:18)

> **"The thief (Satan) comes only to steal and kill and destroy; but I (Jesus) have come that they may have life and have it to the full."** (John 10:10)

Over the years, my prophetic voice had been silenced so much that if I wanted to speak to even just a few people in a room, my whole body would start trembling and my throat would constrict so tightly I could hardly talk. I joined toastmasters to overcome this fear. It took a year to finally rally the courage I needed to get up and make a speech there. It was a resounding success, and I got the award for the night! I know the award was always given to the newbies, but hey, I'd take it. I would take whatever I could at that point.

The Victory Crown

But whenever things are going well, Satan loves to use the closest person to me to pull me down and keep me crippled with fear.

My husband picked me up from toastmasters and I was delighted to have won the award for the night. Finally, I was overcoming fear. But within a couple of minutes of driving, Satan again used my husband to strike terror straight back into my heart. He suddenly started driving on the opposite side of a wet and winding road for no reason, (this had been ongoing torment for me). After heated words, I finally said, let me out and he promptly told me,

"What's wrong with you? Get out then!"

It was 10pm at night, raining and in a dark bushy area far from home, but I gladly hopped out, and he gladly put me out.

When he sped off, I can honestly say I felt in control at last. I was not scared at all as Jesus was walking right beside me. Even though it was a long way home, I thought I would much rather walk in this rain than ever get back in the car with him again. He came back about fifteen minutes later, and of course God instructed me to go with him, but only after I made it truly clear to him that I would never put up with that behaviour ever again. I never received an apology, and my thoughts were that you wouldn't even do that to a dog.

What's wrong with you? Those words rang in my ear's day and night, until even I thought there was something wrong with me. I knew I was far from perfect, but who wasn't?

I worried that people would see this 'Christian marriage' and it would turn them off being a Christian for sure. I also knew it wasn't good for my children to keep seeing it either. Something had to give!

Boundaries Bring Break Through

With his fidelity in question, one night when I couldn't bear it anymore, Jesus stood beside my bed, took me by the hand and led me out into the lounge room. It was about 1am. I begged him to give me a word about my marriage and tell me what to do. I knew I couldn't go on living in a partnership where there was no peace. I said to God that I would open the bible and whatever it said to do, I would do. I felt an anointing wash over me from my head to my toes and when I opened it up it said:

> **"Don't be teamed with those who do not love the Lord, for what do the people of God have in common with the people of sin? How can light live with darkness? And what harmony can there be between Christ and the devil? How can a Christian be a partner with one who doesn't believe? And what union can there be between God's Temple and idols? That is why the Lord has said, leave them; separate yourselves from them; don't touch their filthy things, and I will welcome you, and be a Father to you, and you will be my sons and daughters."**
> (2 Corinthians 6:14-18 {Parts of})

After deep discussions with my pastor and then with my husband, he decided to leave. Just before he had left the marital home, we were talking and something came up about other women and he was quite smug about it. I said,

"You can't just walk out on a family and think that's going to be ok," but he just smirked and mocked me with a big smile.

That mocking reminded me of a word that God had given me to give to him a couple of weeks prior. As it was the first bad word I'd ever got for someone, I was very hesitant. But I knew this was the time to give it to him. I advised him that whether it was spiritual or physical death, I felt the Lord say,

The Victory Crown

"The time has come to get your affairs in order and don't bother trying to buy and sell property. Pack up your things, I've seen the things that were done and I'm sick of the behaviour and the pride." (Ezekial 7 {Parts of})

After the mocking, I walked into the bathroom feeling absolutely humiliated, as I'd given him over 22 years of my life and three beautiful children. So I said to God,

"You have seen everything over the last 22 years and what has been going on. He is now mocking me in the most hurtful way and now he is all yours! It is finished."

Then I heard God say loudly, "YAY FINALLY!" And then He showed me a small artillery soldier (me) being pushed aside and replaced by a big army tank (God) rolling its way in, ready for war. I thought to myself, he's in big trouble now! I also learnt in that moment that I had been doing it all in my own strength for all those years, and how I must have been in God's way. All I could think was, *man, he's in SO much trouble now!*

Within a couple of hours of that word being spoken, he was bedridden with 40-degree temperature and a major health issue presented itself. He was hospitalised and in an extreme state of sickness. They couldn't bring his temperature down and had to put him on a drip. Day after day, they couldn't stop the issue and his temperature remained extremely high. He was losing weight rapidly and put in isolation. The doctors did not know what was wrong, as he didn't respond to anything they were using. He thought he was going to die. Within the week, they'd flown in special antibiotics which finally worked.

Many people were praying for him and over a period of a few weeks, he recovered. He seemed to have a brief turn-around but unfortunately, the trust had been broken and all the initial underlying problems were still very much present.

God wasn't trying to break up my family. What He was really doing was setting me free from the spirit of fear that had entwined itself around me like a chain that was choking me. Thankfully, I knew what to do and asked God to remove it from me.

> **"So, if the Son sets you free, you will be free indeed."**
> (John 8:36)

The Husband Idol

Just after God revealed this stronghold over me, there came another revelation straight away. I was talking with a friend one day and I saw God's face come down between us. I saw His mouth clearly say to me,

"Your husband is an idol in your life."

That stunned me! I stopped what I was doing and in that moment He showed me that all my focus was constantly on my husband and that I had no time to spend with Him. I realised it was so true! That's when God the husband, stepped in.

> **"Fear not; you will no longer live in shame. The shame of your youth and the sorrows of widowhood will be remembered no more, for your Creator will be your husband. The Lord Almighty is his name! He is your Redeemer, the Holy One of Israel, the God of all the earth."** (Isaiah 54:4-5)

Chapter 11

Nakedness Is Intimacy

God My Husband

I had often heard the saying that "God is our husband, and we are His bride," but I didn't know what that meant until my husband left home.

It finally sank in when he separated our joint bank accounts after twenty-two years. Knowing that the following day was his pay day and that nothing was going to go into our bank account, brought a terrible sadness to my heart. I knew then that it was really happening. I worried about what I was going to do financially, but thankfully I had learnt from past situations, and knew exactly what to do. Immediately I turned to God my husband and asked Him if He could put a large lump sum of money into my bank account to help me. At the time, I knew of absolutely no way that any money could come in from anywhere at all, so it seemed like an impossible thing to happen, but as Jesus said,

"What do you mean, 'If I can?' Jesus asked. 'Anything is possible if a person believes.' The father instantly replied, 'I do believe, but help me not to doubt!'" (Mark 9:23-24)

Miracle Money

The next day when I looked in my bank account, I was expecting to see not a lot in there, but something looked strange. I had just purchased a family car for $9,100 as a cash buyer, but it was back in there. I looked again and again and there was $9,300 placed in my account. I knew that wasn't possible for the money from the purchase of the car to go back into my account as I had paid cash. So where did this money come from? I was shocked and thought there must be a mistake.

After doing some investigations, I discovered it was indeed correct, and everything was legitimate. An absolute miracle had occurred with someone I knew, who had owed me money for over twenty years. The debt had now been paid in full. I knew at that point that God was truly my provider.

I had always heard that God was a husband to the widows (nowadays single mums too), but I was about to find out what that really meant.

> "But I will court her again, and bring her into the wilderness, and speak to her tenderly there. There I will give back her vineyards to her and transform her Valley of Troubles into a Door of Hope. She will respond to me there, singing with joy as in days long ago in her youth, after I had freed her from captivity in Egypt.
>
> In that coming day, says the Lord, she will call me 'My Husband' instead of 'My Master.' I will cause you to forget your idols and their names will not be spoken anymore. Then you will lie down in peace and

safety, unafraid: and I will bind you to me forever with chains of righteousness, justice, love, and mercy. I will betroth you to me in faithfulness and love, and you will really know me then as you never have before."
(Hosea 2:14-20 {Parts of})

As I was reading the passage, I saw myself tightly chained to Him, so close from head to toe. I was so excited as I had never seen this side of God before and I couldn't wait. God was showing me that now my husband had gone, He was stepping in as my husband and that also meant Father to my children.

Spiritual Cleansing Technique

God showed me things I never knew about myself and why I had to go through the breakup with my husband. I didn't realise that from the very beginning of our relationship, when there was infidelity, that I had sworn it would never happen again. I had erected walls inside of me for protection, having been in defence mode for twenty-two years. The walls finally had to come down!

With the techniques I learnt on a spiritual cleansing program, I still like to use them on a weekly or daily basis as it brings much freedom and keeps me on track with God:

1st I Repent of what I have done wrong and name it.

2nd I then ask for forgiveness for it.

3rd I renounce whatever spirit I feel is oppressing my life, for example, spirit of unforgiveness.

4th Then I speak out, "I break it in the name of Jesus," clapping my hands when I say "break".

This method is taken from Ezekiel 21:14-17 when the Lord instructed Ezekiel to prophesy, clap his hands, and then the Lord clapped His hands, and it was finished.

Throne Room of God

I now have a much deeper relationship with my heavenly Father, recently visiting the throne room of God in heaven. I can only try to describe it, but no words can really express its beauty. When I looked up, it seemed to me that the ceiling was awash with endless rainbows of shimmering colours. In this room, God sat on a golden throne, with Jesus and the Holy spirit standing at his side. To either side of God's throne, there were elders seated equally on smaller thrones. I wondered at the little glints of light that would sparkle around the room, like tiny shiny rainbows. They were all the promises that God was making to his people, as their petitions came before Him in the throne room.

> **"At once I was in the spirit, and I saw a throne standing in heaven, with someone seated on it. The one seated there looked like jasper and Ruby, and a rainbow that gleamed like an emerald encircled the throne. Surrounding the throne were twenty-four other thrones, and seated on them were twenty-four elders. They were dressed in white and had crowns of gold on their heads."** (Revelation 4:2-4)

Electric Gold Room in Heaven

I was also taken to heaven recently where not only did I see lush meadows of green grass and beautiful crystal lakes, I also rode a horse with Jesus. We came to a gigantic outer wall of heaven and went through a small door set in its side, which opened onto a golden room. The only way to describe the colour was that it was 'electric' gold and illuminated everywhere. You know when you gently blow on the embers of a fire, they glow with that brilliant 'electric' gold. I could also see men standing around in white clothing, holding and reading large books. As we left the room, we found ourselves in a courtyard, where many children dressed in white came running up to us, hugging Jesus and myself. I was overwhelmed by the love flowing from Him and the children and wept. This visit I describe is now one of many, for which I feel eternally grateful and privileged to have experienced.

> **"Jesus said, 'let the little children come to me, and don't stop them, for the kingdom of heaven belongs to such as these.'"** (Matthew 19:14)

I suppose that explains why I often see God ever so gently give me a big kiss on the cheek in the morning or at night. I asked Him one day,

"Why do you do that?"

"Don't you like to give your children a kiss hello and a kiss goodnight?"

"Of course, I do!"

Fun God

I joke around with Him all the time and He will joke right back. This one day in church, I saw His throne suspended again in the middle of the room and He was sitting up there watching the worship. I asked Him if I could come up and sit with Him, and as quick as anything He replied, "not now darling, Daddy's working."

I cracked up laughing as I knew it was a joke, so I hopped up there anyway and gave Him a big cuddle.

Naked Before God
I was in the bathroom one night and He appeared on his Royal Throne, right when I wanted my privacy. Many times, He would show up in the bathroom and I would very politely tell Him to 'leave' or ask Him to 'turn around' and He usually did, but this time He didn't.

"You right there? A bit of privacy please. Just give me a few ticks of the old clock as I must have a shower."

But no, He just sat there looking right at me. Right at that moment, I heard a scripture being read out on this Abide Christian meditation that I was playing in the background. It said to think about this scripture,

> **"Who shall separate us from the love of Christ? Shall trouble, or hardship, persecution, famine, nakedness, danger, or sword."** (Romans 8:35)

Of course, the 'nakedness' part really spoke to me, as I was in the shower at that very moment. Moving position, I saw Him again and there He was, just sitting on his throne looking directly at me. I was trying to hide from Him and cover myself, but I had no luck, as there was nowhere to hide. I knew at that moment that I had parts of my life that I was hiding from Him, but I was also telling Him not to look at me, as I wasn't as young as I used to be. That didn't deter Him in the slightest. I knew after struggling for a few minutes that I just had to surrender every hidden thing to Him and stand in front of Him naked as a jaybird. I let Him have full access to all my insecurities, and things I didn't even know I was carrying until that moment, and I said,

"Okay, you can have it all."

I did this in great humiliation as I knew He wasn't the only one there, as I could see a multitude around Him and they were looking at me too.

Nakedness Is Intimacy

Embarrassed, I turned around to face the other way when I suddenly realised that Jesus was right behind me in the shower. Although I knew He wouldn't hurt me, I still felt fearful for a split second due to past trauma. Immediately I felt and then saw a beautiful velvety dark blue shiny robe cover me and it was Jesus covering my nakedness with the robe of righteousness. He then fastened an exquisite necklace with priceless gemstones around my neck, whilst placing a golden crown upon my head, adorned with gemstones of all varied sizes, shapes and colours. I couldn't help but cry, feeling his great love and gentleness towards me. I knew the scripture straight away.

> **"And when I passed by again, I saw that you were old enough for love. So I wrapped my cloak around you to cover your nakedness and declared my marriage vows. I made a covenant with you, says the Sovereign Lord, and you became mine. Then I bathed you and washed off your blood and I rubbed fragrant oils into your skin. I gave you expensive clothing of fine linen and silk, beautifully embroidered, and sandals made of fine goatskin leather. I gave lovely jewellery, bracelets, beautiful necklaces, a ring for your nose, earrings for your ears, and a lovely crown for your head. And so you were adorned with gold and silver. Your clothes were made of fine linen and costly fabric."** (Ezekiel 16:8-13)

Jesus Naked on the Cross

God then spoke to me and said,

"This is what happened to Jesus as well."

I could see Jesus fully naked, hanging on the cross with all the people surrounding Him, staring at Him. Also, his Father and all the other people in heaven watching on as He was hanging there dying and beaten to a pulp. God said to me that Jesus was also humiliated in front of not only the multitude of people on earth watching His crucifixion, but He was also naked in front of all the citizens in the heavenly realm. They were also witnesses to the atrocities done to Him. I didn't feel so embarrassed anymore after God showed me what Jesus had gone through. My minor embarrassment was nothing compared to what He went through. Just like Jesus's cloak covered my sins and nakedness in the shower, I knew the cloak really represented His precious blood that covers our sins. His blood that was poured out on the cross that day.

> **"Many were amazed when they saw him – beaten and bloodied, so disfigured one would scarcely know he was a person."** (Isaiah 52:14)

Our relationship went from strength to strength that day. No more hiding things from Him and when He visits me in the bathroom now, it's like *oh well, it doesn't matter that I'm naked*. It's like when two people have been married for years, you get very comfortable around each other. There is nothing to hide anymore.

On the 1st of January 2021, I decided that this was the year of my breakthrough. The previous year, I could have made a million dollars buying property as God wanted to bless me, but I walked away from it. I woke up New Year's Day and spoke aloud,

"This is going to be the best year ever!" I was determined to change my life, but I didn't know how that was going to look.

Dressed to the nines, I invited my children out for lunch and spoke aloud again.

"This is going to be the best year ever."

Nothing was going to stop me this year from wanting to glorify God and finish writing The Victory Crown. I knew very well the power of the tongue.

> **"Death and life are in the power of the tongue, and those who love it will eat its fruit."** (Proverbs 18:21)

We were all so cheerful, but as we were about to walk out the door my phone rang. I got told that my favourite 20 year old brother had accidentally drowned on a camping trip. After trying to comfort everyone, I still spoke out, through floods of tears,

"No! This is still going to be the best year ever in the name of Jesus."

> **"He will wipe every tear from their eyes, and there will be no more death, or sorrow or crying or pain. All these things are gone forever. And the one sitting on the throne said, 'Look, I am making everything new!' and then He said to me, 'write this down, for what I tell you is trustworthy and true.'"** (Revelation 21:4-5)

Over the next few months, I was longing to go over and visit my mother-in-law in New Zealand as she was getting close to leaving this earth. One day, as I was just thinking about it all, I noticed out of the corner of my eye that God was sitting on His throne and listening to me.

I didn't know how I could afford to take everyone on a big trip like that, but within 24 hours I received a phone call from a beautiful godly family who lived in NZ, an hour from the nursing home. She offered to pay for us all to fly over and was happy to put us all up in beautiful accommodation for two weeks, all expenses paid. She had no way of knowing that her offer was a total answer to prayer! I will be forever grateful to them for this opportunity.

My dear mother-in-law Muriel passed away shortly after that trip, but not before she gave her heart to the Lord. A year earlier God had told me to go over and read her the bible. She was powerfully touched by God, so much so that she started speaking out scriptures, and praying a blessing over all my children. She joyfully told me He had now come into her heart and didn't know how she knew the scriptures, even though she had rattled off a half a dozen of them. I was in awe and so grateful that I had obeyed Him and gone over. To this day, it is one of the most powerful conversions I have ever seen of the miracle of salvation.

Worldly Security Gone

I had been wanting to sell my Management Rights Business ever since the separation from my husband. Fear had always stopped me from putting it on the market, as it was not just a business, it was our home as well. There was a huge fear of how I was going to support my children when that income wasn't coming in. Fear of not being able to afford another place to live, fear of business failure again and the list just went on and on and on. Of course, it was Satan trying to keep me bound up not only in fear, but the worries of this world. Thankfully, my heavenly husband stepped in.

God showed up as a groom in a beautiful wedding suit and spoke to me ever so sweetly and said,

"You know how a groom on his wedding day deeply loves his bride?" and He showed me a man with an undying love for his bride.

"Yes I do."

"That's how much I love you all the time. Do you know a groom wants to give his bride absolutely anything he can, as he loves her so much?"

"Yes I do."

"That's what I'm like with you all the time, I want to give you everything all the time."

"Do you?"

"Yes I do."

And with that, I thought to myself, if God loves me that much all the time and wants to give me so much all the time, what on earth am I worried about? I placed my home and business up for sale and told Him, "If you're my husband, I'll leave the rest up to you."

Miracle Home

Finally, I had a contract on my home. I found an incredible eleven-bedroom home on acreage that I had always wanted, and it was super cheap. However, as there was a commercial aspect to some of the property, the bank pulled out on finance only a week before settlement. This left us homeless right before Christmas. I rang the bank several times in disbelief as I didn't even think they could do that, as it had already gone unconditional. They assured me that it was impossible to lend me the money as they only did residential loans. I wanted to cry and so did my children, but I remembered how God had done many miracles in my life and how He could do it again. I had a real peace and joy that God would come through for us.

> **"Our LORD, I will remember the things you have done, your miracles of long ago. I will think about each one of your mighty deeds. Everything you do is right, and no other god compares with you. You alone work miracles, and you have let nations see your mighty power. With your own arm you rescued your people."** (Psalm 77:11-15)

The Victory Crown

It was the 17th of December 2021 and all year I had declared that this was going to be the best year ever, even when I had no home to go too. I just said to the kids and declared aloud that we were still going to get this house, as God is the God of the impossible. I had heard it all before and knew that even though the bank said there was absolutely no way they could help me; I knew by now that anything was indeed possible with God.

> **"But Jesus looked at them and said, with man this is impossible, but with God all things are possible."**
> (Matthew 19:26)

Later that same day I had to go for an emergency PET Scan (all over body scan) as the doctors thought they had found stomach cancer from a CT Scan earlier that week (so you could say it was just a tad stressful), but I put my trust in the Lord and told Him, "I hand my life over to you, no matter the test results."

After the scan I was talking with a friend, and she asked if I had sent out the angels? I had not, as with all the upset going on, I had completely forgotten about them. I immediately sent the angels out in the name of Jesus Christ to bring down every demonic strong hold that was stopping my blessing and prayed to God for full healing.

Within about forty minutes of that prayer, I received a call from the bank manager who said that she couldn't stop thinking about me, and that she couldn't promise me anything, but was going to try one more thing to get the loan approved. She advised it was a long shot and might take a couple of days. Each day seemed like an eternity, but on the 12th day of continuous praying, on the 29th of December 2021, I finally got the call from my bank manager. She stated that she had never seen this happen before, but the people higher up in the bank had changed their minds and approved the loan. She said it truly was a miracle.

Nakedness Is Intimacy

What was even more miraculous was that during the waiting time, my mother put us up in her tiny one-bedroom unit and over those few weeks, my love for my mother was totally renewed. God really works in miraculous ways!

Chapter 12

The Victory Crown

Book at Last

> **"Blessed is a man who perseveres under trial; for once he has been approved, he will receive the Crown of Life which the Lord has promised to those who love him."**
> (James 1:12)

Over the last year, I have settled into my wonderful home on an acreage in Queensland's beautiful countryside. I have been able to hold women's retreats and bless family and friends, whilst also spending time away in the presence of God. Celebrating life and just having good old fun playing pool, hot tubbing and sitting in front of the fire.

I found my purpose again after God spoke to me and said,

"Remember who you are, Joanne."

When I recalled everything God had said to me, I announced the words aloud to strengthen myself: "I am the daughter of the Highest God!"

- I am a New Creation in Christ.

- I am a Mighty Warrior in the Kingdom of God.

- I can do all things through Christ who strengthens me.

- I am a daughter of the King and have Royal blood.

- I am more than a conqueror through Christ who loves me.

I have now been set free from past hurts in my marriage and have embarked on a new chapter in my life, that is to do God's work of telling everyone about His wonderful Love and promises.

It is now time to finish what I started. Yes, it took years, but I obviously had a few more things I had to go through, so I could add them to the book before I finished it. I may not be the greatest writer in the world, but really, it's not about how good I am, it's only about how good GOD is. As my favourite preacher, Joyce Meyer, always says, "God would rather a Wildfire, than no fire at all."

When I suffered insecurities where my ability to write this book was concerned, God's response to me was,

"The problem Joanne is that you are too worried about what everyone else is going to think of you. But I say, it's not about what anyone else thinks of you that matters, all that matters is what I think of you, and I think you're pretty great!" He sounded delighted with me.

"Do you?"

"Yes, I sure do! Just always remember Joanne, all that really matters is my Son's Victory and what He did on the cross."

Those words above are for everyone and for anyone who has trouble with worrying about what people think of them. It doesn't matter what other people think of you! All that matters is that He thinks you're pretty great.

Then God said,

"Joanne, this is what you think Victory is; a beautiful big house, green yard, a prestige car, successful financially and emotionally, perfect children all doing what you tell them to do and having the happy, perfect family. That's all well and good, but life's not like that. To me, true Victory is believing in my Son Jesus Christ.

Victory is made up of many little victories along the way. Looking back, you will see how far you have come and every battle and victory you have received until this day. You have four wonderful children that all love Me and are filled with the Holy Spirit. They are healthy, happy, and thriving in life, and I am always with them, and they belong to me."

> **"Everyone who believes that Jesus is the Christ is a child of God. For every child of God defeats this evil world by trusting Christ to give the victory. And the ones who win this battle against the world are the ones who believe that Jesus is the Son of God."** (1 John 5:1-5 {Parts of})

> **"We are more than conquerors through Christ who loves us."** (Romans 8:37)

Eternity in Paradise

He was correct, what more could I want as a mother? Thankfully, there is *so* much more! First and foremost, we have the promise of spending eternity in paradise with God, Jesus, and the Holy Spirit.

Not to mention all the angels, heavenly creatures, loved ones, prophets of old, etc. I can't wait to swim in the River of Life, to run through the luscious green meadows, to walk the streets of gold, and to spend time with Jesus and my heavenly Father for eternity. The Bible says:

> **"As Jesus was dying on the Cross, one of the two criminals that were hanging next to him repented and asked Jesus to remember him when He came into his kingdom. Jesus answered, 'Truly I tell you, today you will be with me in paradise.'"** (Luke 23:43)

So, it's not about how big your house or car is, or how much money you have in your bank account, what labels you wear or what job you have. All that matters is having an intimate relationship with God and the only way you can have that is through Jesus Christ alone.

> **"Jesus answered, 'I am the way, the truth and the life. No-one comes to the Father except through me.'"**
> (John 14:6)

My Greatest Victory is Having Jesus Christ in My Everyday Life

> **"Jesus said, 'Look! Here I stand at the door and knock. If you hear me calling and open the door, I will come in, and we will share a meal as friends. I will invite everyone who is victorious to sit with me on my throne, just as I was victorious and sat with my Father on his throne.'"**
> (Revelation 3:20-21)

Asking Jesus, the Son of God, into your life is the greatest decision you can ever make. A wonderful Saviour that laid down his life for you so that all your sins can be forgiven. A friend that will never leave or forsake you, a constant companion and help in time of need.

The Victory Crown

The things I have mentioned in this book, the encounters I have described and the conversations I've had with God are extraordinary, but this type of intimate relationship is for everyone. This is what God wants with you. We were created to be in an intimate relationship with God, every one of us. Walking and talking daily with Him is what He wants, just like Adam in the very beginning. God visited Adam every day and would walk and talk with him in the gardens. That is intimacy, that is friendship, that is love. That is true Victory!

> **"For God loved the world so much that He gave his one and only son, so that anyone who believes in him shall not die but have eternal life. God did not send his Son into the world to be its judge, but to be its Saviour. Those who believe in the Son are not judged; but those who do not believe have already been judged, because they have not believed in God's only Son."**
> (John 3:16-18)

The Victory Crown

Your Victory Crown

> **"I have fought a good fight, I have finished the race, and I have remained faithful. And now the prize awaits me- the Crown of Righteousness that the Lord, the righteous Judge, will give me on that great day of his return. And the prize is not just for me but for all who eagerly look forward to his glorious return."** (2 Timothy 4:7-8)

Now that you have read of all the wonderful things that God has done for me, I want to offer you an opportunity to find the love and forgiveness that your Heavenly Father wants to give you too. If your

The Victory Crown

desire is to have a deeper intimacy and a closer walk with God, I've got good news for you. If you would like to invite God to come into your life and forgive you of all your sins, wiping the slate clean and giving you a brand new start, this is all you have to do.

> **"For if you confess with your mouth that Jesus is Lord and believe in your heart that God raised him from the dead, you will be saved. For it is by believing in your heart that you are made right with God, and it is by confessing with your mouth that you are saved."**
> (Romans 10:9-10)

All it takes is for you to open your heart, and say aloud –

Dear Lord Jesus,

Thank you for dying on the cross for me. I recognise I am a sinner. Please forgive me for all my sins and come into my life. I receive you as my Lord and Saviour. Please help me to live the rest of my life for you. Thank you Lord for forgiving and saving me and answering my prayer.

Amen.

Congratulations! You have just made the best decision of your life. Welcome! You are now a brand new citizen of heaven.

> **"But we are citizens of heaven, where the Lord Jesus Christ lives. And we are eagerly waiting for him to return as our Saviour."** (Philippians 3:20)

What Do I Do Now?

To start your new journey with God, here are some essential keys to building an intimate relationship with your heavenly Father:

1- PRAY TO GOD & JESUS – Praying is honest communication with your Heavenly Father. We do this by sharing all our emotions with Him. Also praising and thanking Him, confessing our sin, praying for others and asking Him for our needs and desires. When we pray, we engage in loving fellowship with Him. You can talk with Him about anything and everything, and whenever you want. He wants this more than anything!

2- READ THE BIBLE – Reading the Bible every day is so important! It is one of God's ways of talking with you, guiding and encouraging you. It teachers you wisdom and knowledge which is immeasurable. I love the Life application Bible, but there are many different versions, and you can find one that appeals to you. Also read God's Word anytime, anywhere, using apps such as the You Version Bible App.

3- FELLOWSHIP WITH OTHER BELIEVERS – Find a church family. It's not all about going to church, it is about relationship with others and making real connections with like-minded people who love God. Not only do you make new friends, but they help you learn and grow, and truly become family.

4- ASK GOD FOR THE HOLY SPIRIT AND SPEAKING IN TONGUES - Speaking in tongues is the initial evidence of the infilling of the Holy Spirit. God has given us this wonderful spiritual gift to bless, encourage, and refresh us throughout our lives on this earth. It is highly desirable.

5- WATER BAPTISM – Is a public declaration of our faith in Jesus Christ. It is the outward demonstration of the inward transformation that takes place when we receive Him as Lord and Saviour.

6- ASK GOD TO SEE HIM AND HEAR HIM.

7- ASK GOD TO TAKE AWAY ANY DOUBT.

8- LISTEN TO CHRISTIAN MUSIC & PODCASTS - I personally have found Joyce Meyer Ministries' teachings life transforming, and I highly recommend visiting her ministry at joycemeyer.org. Joyce has really helped millions to grow and mature in their walk with God. Focus on the Family is another brilliant ministry, but there are also many other ministries to choose from.

These are just some of the immediate things you can do to build an intimate relationship with God. If you have made this life-changing decision to invite Jesus into your life, I would love to hear from you at Thevictorycrown@gmail.com

Dear Father,

I pray you bless the person who is reading this book and give them exceeding great knowledge and understanding, wisdom and discernment. Please reveal yourself to them and open their eyes to the wonders of your Majesty! May you fill them with your Incredible Love, Peace and Joy, and protect them all the days of their life. I ask this in Jesus' mighty name.

AMEN

KEYS TO VICTORY

1- Love God & Love one another

2- Spend time in God's presence and forgive others

3- Worship Him always

4- Read the Bible every day

5- Ask God for Wisdom & Discernment

6- Be Generous and Honest

7- Develop Healthy Boundaries

8- Pray for and help others

9- Pray for Patience & the Blood of Jesus over you and your family every day

10- Ask God for self-control

About the Author

Joanne Hayward is currently the Company Owner of Hayward Management Rights. Her background includes licenses in property management and sales, Prophetic ministry, Prayer Counselling, Pastoral Care and Hospitality.

Joanne's greatest achievement in life so far is being a hands on mother to her four beautiful children.

Her greatest passion in life is sharing the Good News message that God, Jesus and the Holy Spirit are REAL, and to help others develop an intimate relationship with them.

As Joanne has had many battles to overcome during her lifetime, her heart's desire is to encourage and see people set free from the prison of their past mistakes and receive victory in the toughest of life's situations.

The driving force behind The Victory Crown is to show people you don't have to be perfect to meet God and to receive Eternal Life.

Testimonials

Myself and my wife Trish have known Joanne Hayward for about 8 years and we consider her a close friend. I also know her on a professional level. Joanne is a very gifted prophet and has always had a deep insight into the ways of God, for us personally and into the lives of others. I know her insight into the ways of the Holy spirit, and into people's lives, will no doubt come out in this book.

Pastor Craig Watts

Dear Reader, Wow! Joanne has finally written her faithful testimony for everyone to read. My family and I have grown a close friendship with Joanne Hayward over the 12years we have known each other. Her strong faith and visitations face to face with Jesus have encouraged us and built up our own faith immensely. She shared her support freely through her God given wisdom. This book will bring glory to God.

Petra Smedley, Teacher Aide.

As Joanne's big sister, I have known her all her life and bear witness to both the mess, the millions, and a lot of the amazing miracles that have taken place in her life since she first heard the message of the gospel. Joanne is one of the most genuine, caring, loving and generous people I have ever known. Seeking no glory for herself, I have watched her run herself ragged helping others, and loving people with Christ's love. I have watched Jo chase down the anointing, chase down the blessings and chase down her God. Jo has a unique walk with God that she shares with her readers throughout this book, along with a message of love that will both bless and encourage its readers to seek a deeper walk with him.

Lisa Reynolds - Borradale, Gospel Singer/Songwriter

Bibliography

The Life Application Bible - The Living Bible

The Life Application Study Bible - NLT (New living Translation)

Joyce Meyer Ministries

Notes

The Victory Crown

Notes

www.ingramcontent.com/pod-product-compliance
Lightning Source LLC
Chambersburg PA
CBHW041317110526
44591CB00021B/2814